# COMPLETE

## PRELIMINARY

**Workbook**
**with answers**

**Second edition**

T0306631

**B1**

WITH AUDIO
DOWNLOAD

Caroline Cooke

For the revised exam from 2020

**Cambridge University Press**

www.cambridge.org/elt

**Cambridge Assessment English**

www.cambridgeenglish.org

Information on this title: www.cambridge.org/9781108525794

© Cambridge University Press and UCLES 2019

First published 2010
Second edition 2019

20  19  18  17  16  15  14  13  12  11  10  9  8  7  6  5  4  3  2

Printed in Mexico by Editorial Impresora Apolo, S.A. de C.V.

*A catalogue record for this publication is available from the British Library*

ISBN 978-1-108-52579-4 Workbook with answers with Audio Download

# Contents

1   My life and home                    4

2   Making choices                      8

3   Having fun                          12

4   On holiday                          16

5   Different feelings                  20

6   That's entertainment!               24

7   Getting around                      28

8   Influencers                         32

9   Stay fit and healthy                36

10  Looks amazing!                      40

11  The natural world                   44

12  Express yourself!                   48

## Vocabulary extra

1   My life and home                    52

2   Making choices                      53

3   Having fun                          54

4   On holiday                          55

5   Different feelings                  56

6   That's entertainment!               57

7   Getting around                      58

8   Influencers                         59

9   Stay fit and healthy                60

10  Looks amazing!                      61

11  The natural world                   62

12  Express yourself!                   63

Answer key                             64

# 1 My life and home

## Vocabulary

### House and home

**1** Put the letters in order to make words for objects you can find in a house.

1 I don't have a *evdut* on my bed in the summer. It's too hot. ...............................

2 I only use one *olwilp* when I am sleeping. ...............................

3 Put the dirty plates in the *kins* and I'll wash them later. ...............................

4 Don't forget to put the milk back in the *drfeig*. ...............................

5 We often heat up food in the *vwiromace* when we don't have time to cook. ...............................

6 Have you got a *elwot* I can use to dry my hands? ...............................

7 I looked in the *rorimr* to see if my make-up was all right. ...............................

8 I turned on the hot *pta*, but the water was cold! ...............................

## Prepositions of time and place

**2** Complete the sentences with *in*, *on* or *at*.

1 I'll see you ............... six o'clock outside the cinema.

2 I love to go hiking ............... spring when it's not too hot.

3 You'll find the toilets down the corridor ............... the right.

4 We played tennis ............... the park.

5 I arrived late ............... the evening after a long day at work.

6 I left my bus pass ............... home, so I paid the fare in cash.

7 There's a clock ............... the wall in the kitchen.

8 She usually eats with her family ............... her birthday.

## Countable and uncountable nouns

**3** Put the words in the correct column.

> beach  bus  cooker  day  electricity  floor  food
> friend  furniture  game  hall  homework  house
> make-up  money  rain  shampoo  space
> tap  time

| Countable | Uncountable |
|---|---|
|  |  |

## Reading Part 5

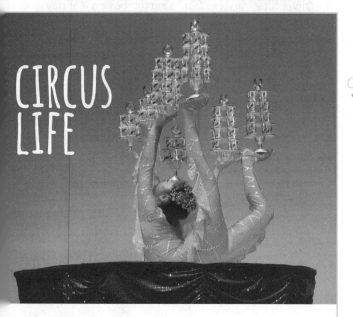

# CIRCUS LIFE

Sue Lee is an acrobat. She works in a circus that travels around the world, so she stays in many different cities. Her daily **(1)** .............................. is nearly always the same. Most days, she gets up at 7 o'clock, has breakfast and gets **(2)** .............................. to go to training. Depending on the city she is in, she walks or takes the bus to the theatre where that evening's **(3)** .............................. takes place.

Normally, Sue does eight or nine shows a week, sometimes two a day, so it's **(4)** .............................. work. She has to make sure she has a healthy **(5)** .............................., so she eats a lot of fruit, vegetables and proteins to keep her body strong. In the afternoon, she has some free time and usually tries to **(6)** .............................. in touch with family or friends on her laptop, although when she's in some countries the time difference can make it difficult.

**1** For each question, choose the correct answer.

| | **A** | **B** | **C** | **D** |
|---|---|---|---|---|
| **1** | way | custom | routine | habit |
| **2** | ready | better | early | right |
| **3** | play | audience | presentation | performance |
| **4** | heavy | hard | huge | long |
| **5** | food | dish | diet | supply |
| **6** | make | get | hold | go |

## Listening Part 2

**1** For each question, choose the correct answer.

**1** You will hear a mother and her son talking about his old school books.
What do they decide to do with his books?
**A** put them away in his bedroom
**B** give them to someone else
**C** throw them away

**2** You will hear a boy telling his friend about helping at home.
How does he feel about it?
**A** excited by the idea
**B** annoyed that his brother doesn't help
**C** confident that it won't take long

**3** You will hear two college students talking about a trip.
The man says he will miss the trip because
**A** he's going away with his parents.
**B** he hasn't got the right equipment.
**C** he has made a mistake with the date.

**4** You will hear two friends talking about a TV series.
What does the man like about the series?
**A** It shows realistic family situations.
**B** It has good actors.
**C** It had a surprising ending.

**5** You will hear a woman talking to a friend about a house.
What is the problem with the woman's new house?
**A** It's too far from her work.
**B** There are too few bedrooms.
**C** There's no space for her car.

**6** You will hear two friends talking about a shopping centre.
They agree that
**A** it has a good variety of shops.
**B** it has improved the town.
**C** it's in a convenient location.

# 1

## Grammar

### Frequency adverbs

**1** Put the words in order to make sentences.

1 in / eat / They / restaurant / a / occasionally

..........................................................................

2 year / go / once / I / skiing / a

..........................................................................

3 takes / hardly / on / He / holiday / photos / ever

..........................................................................

4 a / I / good / day / every / breakfast / eat

..........................................................................

5 abroad / She / go / often / holiday / doesn't / on

..........................................................................

6 every / Some / read / the / people / newspaper / day / almost

..........................................................................

..........................................................................

7 take / days / dog / I / the / park / to / my / most

..........................................................................

..........................................................................

8 mornings / They / home / never / the / are / at / in

..........................................................................

..........................................................................

### *a few, a bit of, many, much, a lot of* and *lots of*

**2** Choose the correct option.

1 I'd like ............................. butter on my toast, please.

  **a** much    **b** a bit of    **c** a few

2 There aren't ............................. cushions in the living room.

  **a** few    **b** much    **c** many

3 Have you got ............................. friends from your childhood?

  **a** much    **b** lots    **c** many

4 Only ............................. people bought his record. It wasn't very popular.

  **a** a bit of    **b** many    **c** a few

5 I had to pay ............................. money for my new laptop.

  **a** a few    **b** a lot of    **c** much

6 My sister sings ............................. when she's in the shower.

  **a** a lot    **b** lots of    **c** much

7 I've got ............................. time if you want some help now.

  **a** lots of    **b** much    **c** a few

8 The children didn't have ............................. sugar on their cereal.

  **a** much    **b** many    **c** a few

## Present simple and present continuous

**3** Choose the correct option in *italics*.

1 We can't go out because it *snows / is snowing* today.

2 All the players *know / are knowing* that the match is tomorrow.

3 The supermarket *opens / is opening* at 10 o'clock on Sundays.

4 My sister *hates / is hating* TV programmes about history.

5 Oliver often *misses / is missing* the bus on Monday mornings.

6 Most police officers *wear / are wearing* a uniform for work.

7 My tomato plants *grow / are growing* very quickly this year.

8 My girlfriend *learns / is learning* Japanese at the moment.

9 The weather *gets / is getting* better this month.

10 Some people *watch / are watching* too much TV.

**4** Complete the email with the correct form of the verb in brackets.

Hi Jackie,

Well, here I am in Peru! Yes, I **(1)** ........................................ (spend) a year in Lima as part of my university course. I **(2)** ........................................ (feel) so lucky because it's a fantastic opportunity. I **(3)** ........................................ (have) an apartment in the city centre with two other girls, and we **(4)** ........................................ (go) to classes on foot because it's very close to the university.

Here, the university courses **(5)** ........................................ (start) in April, which is the end of summer, and they **(6)** ........................................ (finish) in February. I **(7)** ........................................ (attend) classes Monday to Friday. But today is Saturday, so I **(8)** ........................................ (not / study). Instead, I **(9)** ........................................ (sit) in the kitchen writing emails. I **(10)** ........................................ (not / have) much free time in the week because this month we **(11)** ........................................ (do) a project, which **(12)** ........................................ (mean) we have to do a lot of extra work in the evenings. At the moment, I **(13)** ........................................ (take) Spanish classes as well. What **(14)** ........................................ (you / do) this year? **(15)** ........................................ (you / want) to come and visit me?

Write soon!
Love,
Sammy

## Writing Part 1

**Exam advice**

- Remember there are four points you have to answer in the email. Make sure you answer each one and add enough information about each point so that your email is about 100 words. Use words like *because*, *so* or *and*.
- You can use questions to make suggestions, give invitations or ask for further information.

**1** Match the beginnings and endings of the sentences.

1 Let's meet at 10 o'clock,
2 Wednesday is the best day
3 The park is very big,
4 The beach is a great idea

a so we can have a good walk there.
b because I love swimming in the sea.
c because I don't have yoga classes that afternoon.
d so we have time to buy some food first.

**2** Complete the table with the questions.

| Inviting |
|---|
|  |

| Suggesting |
|---|
|  |

| Asking for information |
|---|
|  |

1 Would you like to come to my party?
2 Which is the best place to visit?
3 Shall we go to the exhibition?
4 Do you want to go to the theatre tonight?
5 What kind of films do you like?
6 Why don't we have a barbecue?

**3** Read this email from your English-speaking friend Robin, and the notes you have made. Write your answer in about 100 words.

**To:**
**From:** Robin

Hi,

I'm writing with some great news. My friend Jack says I can use his apartment on the coast in the first two weeks of August. There's space for two people. Would you like to come? — *Yes, thanks!*

I've only got one week's holiday, so which of those two weeks in August would be best for you? — *Say which and why*

The house is near the beach and the weather will be hot. What kind of activities should we do at the beach? — *Tell Robin*

We don't have to pay for the apartment, but I'd like to get Jack a present to say thank you. I thought maybe something for the house. What could we get him? — *Suggest ...*

Lots of love,
Robin

# 2 Making choices

## Vocabulary

**1** Complete the sentences with words from the box.

> fail  learn  lose  miss  pass  set off
> study  take  teach  work

1 In my final year at university, I have to ............................... six exams. If I ............................... them all, I'll get my degree.

2 I was very nervous, so I thought I was going to ............................... my driving test.

3 I only ............................... part-time because I'm a student. I ............................... at university in the mornings. Then I ............................... little children maths in the afternoon. I think they ............................... a lot with me.

4 I can't find my bus pass. I hope I didn't ............................... it yesterday.

5 I ............................... for work at 7 o'clock because if I leave later, I ............................... the train.

### do, earn, make, spend, take and win

**2** Exam candidates often make mistakes with vocabulary. Underline and correct one vocabulary mistake in each sentence.

1 Karen prefers to spend the money she wins from her job on travelling rather than clothes.

..............................................................................................

2 It's not easy for me to do new friends nowadays because I work from home.

..............................................................................................

3 I earn a lot of money on travelling to work each month.

..............................................................................................

4 Harry made his best, but he didn't get the job.

..............................................................................................

5 I have to do a lot of time writing emails at work.

..............................................................................................

6 The journey to work spent me a long time today because the traffic was terrible.

..............................................................................................

7 It makes me a long time to get to the office.

..............................................................................................

8 I was delighted when I earned first prize in the short-story competition.

..............................................................................................

## Reading Part 6

- Read the whole text first before you complete any of the gaps.
- The missing words are almost always 'grammatical' words, e.g. articles (*a, the*), auxiliary verbs (*have/has, is/was, do/does*, etc), pronouns (*it, them, him, my,* etc), prepositions (*in, at, for,* etc) or linking words (*but, when, if*, etc).

**Exam advice**

**1** For each question, write the correct word. Write one word in each gap.

**What are you doing now you've finished university?**

**My first job**

I got the job in environmental research a couple **(1)** ............................... months after finishing my degree.
I had applied **(2)** ............................... several jobs in different companies, but this was the one I really wanted, so I was delighted.

Working in an environmental organisation is an amazing experience. I am a research assistant in the laboratory, working with a great team. Since I started here, I **(3)** ............................... met a lot of interesting people who are studying the effect of climate change on our planet.

I think that protecting the environment is one of **(4)** ............................... most important issues in our world today, and I want to help in any way I can, so this is a great opportunity for me. To begin with I don't have a very high salary, **(5)** ............................... I'm happy to get the experience. They are also going to pay for **(6)** ............................... to take some courses to learn more.

## Grammar

### Past simple

**1** Complete the dialogues with the correct past simple form of the verbs in the box. You need to use some of the verbs more than once.

> do   earn   get   go   have
> make   meet   spend   take

**1** **A:** Yesterday, I ............................ three hours working on that report for my boss. Did you finish your work?

**B:** Yes, but it ............................ me a long time, too. ............................ you ............................ to the gym after work?

**A:** No, I ............................ (not) time.

**2** **A:** My sister ............................ a music degree from London University last year, and now she plays in an orchestra.

**B:** ............................ she ............................ a lot of money when she started?

**A:** No, but she ............................ fun.

**3** **A:** I ............................ to Germany for a summer course last July.

**B:** ............................ you ............................ many friends?

**A:** Yes, I ............................ people from lots of different countries.

**4** **A:** I ............................ (not) very well in the marketing exam last week. I know I ............................ a lot of mistakes.

**B:** That's because you ............................ (not) much time revising.

**A:** I know. I thought I ............................ a good memory, but I was wrong!

### Past simple and past continuous, *used to*

**2** Choose the correct option in *italics*.

**1** I *used to enjoy / was enjoying* going to clubs when I was younger, but now I find them very noisy.

**2** He *gave / was giving* a presentation in the communication skills class when the computer *stopped / was stopping* working.

**3** *Did you spend / Were you spending* a lot of money when you were on holiday last year?

**4** It *was raining / used to rain* when we left the house, but later the sun *came / was coming* out.

**5** I *talked / was talking* on my phone when I *received / was receiving* a text.

**6** My parents *didn't use to let / weren't letting* me go out on school days, even when I was 17.

**7** The scientist *concentrated / was concentrating* so hard that he *didn't realise / wasn't realising* it was late.

**8** We *decided / were deciding* to have a cup of coffee while we *used to shop / were shopping* in the city centre.

**3** Complete the text with the verbs in brackets in the past simple or past continuous.

## NEVER MIND THE WEATHER!

It was the trip of a lifetime. We **(1)** ............................ (set off) from the first hostel early in the morning to walk the first stage on a path which went up and down mountains for about 25km. It was a beautiful day, the sun **(2)** ............................ (shine) and the countryside **(3)** ............................ (look) beautiful. We went up a steep hill and soon we **(4)** ............................ (arrive) at a small bridge over a river. The water **(5)** ............................ (run) fast and clean. It also **(6)** ............................ (feel) very cold because it came down from the snowy mountains above.

After about two hours, we **(7)** ............................ (stop) for a rest and sat down. Then, I **(8)** ............................ (notice) some dark clouds **(9)** ............................ (come) in from the north, so we decided to continue quickly. But we **(10)** ............................ (not walk) fast enough, and it **(11)** ............................ (begin) raining. It **(12)** ............................ (still rain) four hours later when we finally arrived at our destination, completely wet. It **(13)** ............................ (not matter) because we **(14)** ............................ (have) dry clothes in our bags and we **(15)** ............................ (feel) amazing after completing our first day.

## Listening Part 1

> • Look at the question and the three pictures for each question. Think about the words you will hear.
>
> • Choose your answer the first time you listen. Then, check it carefully when you listen again.
>
> • Don't spend too long on an answer if you're not sure – choose an answer and move on to the next question.

**Exam advice**

**1** For each question, choose the correct answer.

**03**

**1** What job does the student want to do after university?

**2** Where are the woman's glasses?

**3** When do the students have to give their final presentation?

| A | | B | | C | |
|---|---|---|---|---|---|
| ...ay | Thursday | ...ay | Thursday *presentation* | ...ay | Thursday |
| Monday | Friday | Monday | Friday | Monday | Friday *presentation* |
| Tuesday *presentation* | Saturday | Tuesday | Saturday | Tuesday | Saturday |
| Wednesday | Sanday | Wednesday | Sanday | Wednesday | Sanday |

**4** Which activity does the man recommend?

A   B   C

**5** What did they do when it started to rain?

A   B   C

**6** What was the first prize in the competition?

A   B   C

**7** Why did the man go to bed late?

A   B   C

## Writing Part 2 (An article)

**Exam advice**

- Read the instructions carefully and decide who you are writing the article for.
- Look at the title and the questions and think what sort of things you could write that would answer the questions in the exam task.

**1** Read the task below. What information do you need to include in your answer?

You see this notice in an international English-language magazine.

---

**We want your opinion!**

**<u>What makes a good university or college?</u>**

Is it the teachers, the facilities or something else?

What social activities should a good university or college offer?

Tell us what you think!

**Write an article answering these questions and we will publish the most interesting articles in our magazine.**

---

Write your **article**.

**2** Look at Charlie's ideas below. Tick (✓) the ideas that answer the questions.

| What makes a good university or college? | What kind of social activities should a good university or college offer? |
|---|---|
| 1  interesting lectures | 5  sports facilities for when students want a break |
| 2  the possibility to live at home | 6  you need good grades to study there |
| 3  up-to-date equipment that you will find in modern businesses | 7  give people the chance to develop their hobbies |
| 4  practical courses as well as classes about theory | 8  clubs and concerts help students relax after studying |

**3** Make a list of your own ideas in the table below.

| What makes a good university or college? | What kind of social activities should a good university or college offer? |
|---|---|
|  |  |

**4** Complete the sentences with the words from the box.

agree   opinion   sure   think

1  In my ............................... we should choose according to the standard of teaching.
2  I'm ............................... that going to university includes more than just studying.
3  I don't ............................... that we should worry about sports facilities.
4  I ............................... with you. It's a good idea to have a year studying abroad.

**5** Now write your answer to the task in Exercise 1 in about 100 words.

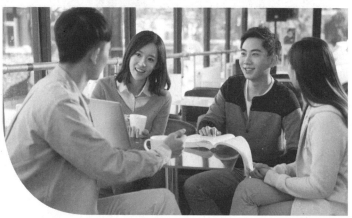

# 3 Having fun

> • Be careful with negative verb forms or words that have opposite meanings to those in the question. The options may not be correct because they say the opposite of the information in the text.
>
> • Check your answer by trying to work out what's wrong with the others.

**Exam advice**

Jason talks about **GEOCACHING**

People often say technology is unhealthy because so much time is spent sitting watching a screen, but we can combine exercise with using our phones. Geocaching is a great hobby, where you have to try to find hidden containers in the countryside from information that's posted on the internet by other people. Using an app with a map, you can find the location and race your friends to be the first one there and open the container. It's surprising what people leave inside, and there are some hiding places that I would never have thought of.

My initial experience with geocaching was quite an adventure. My whole group was new to the activity, so it wasn't the best-planned trip. The first problem was with technology, of course. My phone didn't have enough memory to download the app, so I ended up having to share with a friend. This meant that either we had to go at the same speed or that one of us got left behind without being able to join in. That one was usually me when I felt tired and needed to rest.

Since then, I have become quite a fan and I even create my own geocaches, where I put objects such as badges, key rings or even sometimes money, for others to find. There's a real community of people who are into playing. They have set up clubs to get together to play and then go for a meal afterwards. There are numerous blogs about the best gifts to replace anything you take or where there might be a new geocache. You might wonder what the farmers and others who live in the countryside think about this invasion of hunters, but in general they seem quite happy as long as the visitors respect the environment and their privacy.

So, if you want to try something new and get out in the fresh air, get out your phone, call a few friends and take them for a day's hunting. It's perfect for families with children, especially those who protest when their parents try to get them off their screens and outside. The motivation of going from one hiding place to another as fast as possible means that they walk a long way without realising, and they even enjoy spending time with their parents!

**1** Read the text. For each question, choose the correct answer.

**1** Jason thinks geocaching
   A helps people to use technology.
   B takes a long time to arrange.
   C shows people have a lot of imagination.
   D prepares people for races:

**2** Jason says the first time he went geocaching
   A he had difficulties remembering where to go.
   B he forgot to take some essential equipment.
   C the people he went with were more experienced than he was.
   D he couldn't participate as much as he wanted to.

**3** Geocache players
   A need to be very organised.
   B exchange ideas about the game.
   C often live in the countryside.
   D want to protect nature.

**4** Jason suggests that geocaching
   A is good for relationships.
   B is best for small groups of people.
   C doesn't work well in the city.
   D isn't suitable for lazy people.

**5** What might Jason say to a friend who wants to try geocaching?
   A You'll need a good map and be careful of people who don't like you to walk on their land.
   B Make sure you have the right equipment and don't forget to bring some gifts to put in the boxes.
   C It's important to win and you'll get some amazing prizes if you are able to find the right locations.
   D If you don't like walking, you'll find this boring, but you can always chat to your friends online and eat good food.

## Vocabulary

### Prepositions of place

**1** Look at the picture and complete the sentences with a preposition.

**1** The man is ............................ the window.

**2** The clock is ............................ the poster.

**3** The cupboard is ............................ the right of the window.

**4** The umbrellas are ............................ the door.

**5** The radiator is ............................ the window.

**6** A plant is ............................ the two desk lamps.

**7** There is a cupboard with books ............................ .

**8** There are some boxes ............................ the corner.

### Phrasal verbs

**2** Replace the words in bold with a phrasal verb from the box in the correct form.

> give up   go on   hang on   join in   look after
> run out of   set off   sign up

**1** We **had no more** milk, so I went to the supermarket.
............................

**2** If you want to **put your name down** for the course, you have to go online. ............................

**3** Can you **wait** a minute? I'm nearly ready. ............................

**4** Would you like to **be part of** the study group? We meet on Wednesdays. ............................

**5** I decided to **stop** playing tennis because I hurt my arm. ............................

**6** We **left home** at 6 o'clock to get to the airport at 7.30. ............................

**7** Do you want to **continue** working or shall we have a break? ............................

**8** Can you **take care of** my plants when I go on holiday? ............................

### People's hobbies

**3** Choose the correct option in *italics* and complete the sentences with the person who has the hobby.

**1** A person who *rides / plays* a bicycle is called a ............................ .

**2** A person who *plays / does* chess is called a ............................ .

**3** A person who *makes / takes* photographs is called a ............................ .

**4** A person who *goes / plays* diving is called a ............................ .

**5** A person who *plays / touches* a musical instrument is called a ............................ .

## Listening Part 4

**1** For each question, choose the correct answer. You will hear a radio interview with a young magician called Megan.

**1** Megan decided to become a magician
  **A** when she saw a magician perform.
  **B** because her friends encouraged her.
  **C** after she joined a magician's club.

**2** At the magic club, Megan
  **A** didn't get to perform many new tricks.
  **B** wasn't a typical member of the group.
  **C** came first in a competition.

**3** What does Megan say about her work in an office?
  **A** She had to study hard to get her job.
  **B** She doesn't mind not earning much money.
  **C** She doesn't have time to do much magic.

**4** What is Megan most proud of?
  **A** getting a degree in conservation
  **B** becoming secretary of The Magic Circle
  **C** becoming a vet after university

**5** What does Megan say about the magic she performs?
  **A** She talks very fast while she does her tricks.
  **B** She doesn't use any sound.
  **C** She uses a lot of movement.

**6** How does Megan feel about her life now?
  **A** pleased because she can do all the things she likes
  **B** worried because she needs to make a decision
  **C** confident that she will be more successful in the future

## Grammar

### Verbs followed by *to* or *-ing*

**1** Choose the correct option in *italics*.

**1** I missed *to be / being* with my brother when he went to live abroad.

**2** The friends agreed *to meet / meeting* outside the station before they went to the party.

**3** Brad hopes *to go / going* skiing next winter.

**4** My mother learnt *to drive / driving* when she was 50!

**5** Hannah doesn't feel like *to do / doing* much today.

**6** Have you finished *to read / reading* that article yet?

**7** I don't mind *to see / seeing* that film again. It was excellent.

**8** You should practise *to speak / speaking* in front of a mirror before you give your presentation.

**9** Would you like *to come / coming* to my house this afternoon?

**2** Choose the correct sentence, a or b.

**1 a** Don't forget to wear your helmet when you're cycling!
  **b** Don't forget wearing your helmet when you're cycling!

**2 a** I remember my grandma to teach me how to make biscuits.
  **b** I remember my grandma teaching me how to make biscuits.

**3 a** Luckily, I remembered putting on sun cream when I went sunbathing yesterday.
  **b** Luckily, I remembered to put on sun cream when I went sunbathing yesterday.

**4 a** I'll never forget going diving in the sea for the first time!
  **b** I'll never forget to go diving in the sea for the first time!

**3** Complete the conversation between three friends with the verb in brackets in the correct form, *to* + infinitive or *–ing*.

**Katie:** OK, everyone. We need to finalise the plans for going to the festival this weekend. What time shall we leave?

**Ben:** I suggest **(1)** ........................... (meet) at the car park at 10 o'clock.

**Katie:** That's perfect. We'll have time to go shopping to get some food for the journey. Do you fancy **(2)** ........................... (take) sandwiches? Or we could stop at a café on the way.

**Ben:** I can't afford **(3)** ........................... (eat) in a café. Let's get bread and cheese to make our own sandwiches.

**Katie:** OK. Did you remember **(4)** ........................... (ask) Lily if we can borrow her tent?

**Ben:** Oh no, I'll send her a text now. I'm sure she'll say yes.

**Katie:** Liam, you promised **(5)** ........................... (bring) the programme so we can plan which bands to see.

**Liam:** Oh no! ..., I forgot **(6)** ........................... (put) it in my bag.

**Katie:** Typical! So we need to make a list of things to take. Do you remember **(7)** ........................... (go) to a festival last year when it rained, and no one had a raincoat?

**Ben:** But we still enjoyed **(8)** ........................... (dance) in the rain, didn't we? Do we *have* to be so organised?

## Writing Part 2 (A story)

**Exam advice**

- The story must follow on from the sentence you are given. Think carefully about a possible situation before you start writing.
- Don't change the sentence you are given.
- Plan your story. Make notes about what happens first, second, third, etc. before you start writing.

**1** Read the exam task and answer the questions with your own ideas.

> Your English teacher has asked you to write a story. Your story must begin with this sentence.
>
> *I opened the door and was amazed by what I saw.*

1 Where was the door? In a house / a hotel / an office? In another place?
2 What did you see when you opened the door?
3 Why was it amazing?
4 What did you do?

**2** Look at the beginning of two answers to this question. Which one follows the sentence in Exercise 1 better?

**A** I opened the door and was amazed by what I saw. The restaurant was full of people, but no one was moving! I closed the door and opened it again, but they were all frozen.

**B** I opened the door and was amazed by what I saw. My sister was sitting on the sofa and my dog was sleeping on the floor. I went into the living room and sat down to watch TV.

**3** Write two or three sentences to start your story with this sentence. Use the questions below to help you.

*I walked into the room and everyone stopped talking.*

1 Where was the room?
2 Who was in the room?
3 Why did they stop talking?
4 What did you do?

**4** Make notes about how the story continued. Use these ideas.

- What happened next?
- What did you say?
- What happened in the end?

**5** Now, write the story. Write about 100 words.

# 4 On holiday

## Grammar

### big and enormous

**1** Choose the correct option in *italics*.

1 The water in the lake is absolutely *cold / freezing*.
2 Hiking all day is *very / totally* exhausting.
3 We visited an *extremely / absolutely* fascinating sealife centre, which even had sharks.
4 The new earphones were *extremely / totally* small.
5 We gave the theme park a very *terrible / bad* review.

### Comparative and superlative adjectives, (not) as … as

**2** Complete the sentences with the correct form of the adjective in brackets.

1 The ............................... (good) way to get to the island is by boat.
2 I prefer to walk because it's as ........................... (quick) as the bus.
3 Using Google maps is the ........................... (easy) way to get directions.
4 Why are you late? I expected you to be here ........................... (early).
5 Health and happiness are ........................... (important) than money.
6 That was the ........................... (bad) storm in ten years.

**3** Exam candidates often make mistakes with comparatives and superlatives.
Underline and correct one mistake in each sentence.

1 The meals in the USA are more bigger than at home.
..........................................................
2 The wildlife in the desert was more interesting that I imagined. ........................................
3 The cruise ship was one of the larger in the world.
..........................................................
4 It took us as longer to get to the station as to the airport. ........................................
5 One of the best thing about the holiday was the weather. ........................................

**4** Complete the sentences with the correct form of the adjective in brackets and words from the box.

> as … as   a bit   a little   a lot
> far   much   slightly   than

**Sunshine Hotel**
500€ a night 200 rooms
200 m from the beach
breakfast from 6–9 am
2 hours from airport

**∽∽∽ The Grand Hotel ∽∽∽**

- 50€ a night
- 200 rooms
- 1 km from the beach
- breakfast from 9–11 am
- 15 mins from airport

**TIPTOP HOTEL**
55€ a night  20 rooms
200 m from the beach
no breakfast available
20 mins from airport

1 The Tiptop Hotel is ........................... the Sunshine Hotel. (small)
2 The Sunshine Hotel isn't ........................... from the beach ........................... the Grand Hotel. (far)
3 The Sunshine Hotel is ........................... the Grand Hotel. (expensive)
4 The Sunshine Hotel is ........................... the Grand Hotel. (big)
5 It takes ........................... to get to the Tiptop Hotel from the airport ........................... the Grand Hotel. (long)
6 The Grand Hotel serves breakfast ........................... ........................... the Sunshine Hotel. (late)
7 The Tiptop Hotel is ........................... the beach ........................... the Grand Hotel. (near)
8 The Grand Hotel is ........................... the Tiptop Hotel. (cheap)
9 The Grand Hotel isn't ........................... the Tiptop Hotel. (small)

## Reading Part 1

**1** For each question, choose the correct answer.

**1**

# WILDLIFE PARK

**No swimming in the lake**

**Barbecues allowed in the picnic area**

**Take your rubbish home with you**

A  You are allowed to swim in the water.
B  You must throw things away in the park's rubbish bins.
C  You can cook in a special place.

**2**

Hi Emily

Are you ready for the camping trip tomorrow? I've got a tent, but could you pack a torch? Mine's broken – I won't have time to replace it. Don't forget we're leaving early!

Kelly

Kelly wants Emily to

A  remember to bring something for the trip.
B  find something to use for cooking on the trip.
C  leave something they don't need for the trip.

**3**

Hi Larry

I've got a problem with meeting on Friday. What about Saturday instead? There's a much better film on then. I hope you haven't got the tickets yet!

Ollie

A  Ollie will buy the tickets for the cinema.
B  Ollie wants to go to the cinema on a different day.
C  Ollie is confirming that they will see the same film as previously planned.

**4**

## ENTRY FREE FOR LOCAL RESIDENTS OR FOR VISITORS UNDER EIGHTEEN OR OVER SIXTY-FIVE
## IDENTIFICATION NECESSARY FOR ALL

A  If you live in the area, you can go in without paying.
B  Everyone over eighteen has to pay to go in.
C  Certain people need to show a document for free entry.

**5**

Tessa

Have you tried that restaurant in the square next to the bank? I wouldn't go to the one near the bridge. The food can be expensive there, and it's not very tasty.

Jake

A  Jake is recommending the food at the restaurant near the bridge.
B  Jake is telling Tessa to try the food in several restaurants.
C  Jake is asking Tessa what she thinks about the restaurant in the square.

## Vocabulary

### Buildings and places

**1** Match the places with the signs.

1  art gallery
2  department store
3  factory
4  library
5  sports centre
6  fountain
7  town hall
8  stadium

a  **Don't throw rubbish in the water**

b  Temporary exhibition – Landscapes from the 18th century

c  LIFT TO SECOND FLOOR – WOMEN'S CLOTHES

d  Historical novels and non-fiction upstairs

e  ★ Lions vs Bears Champions match – tickets here ★

f  Do not operate the machine without gloves

g  **Council meeting here Friday 8.00 pm**

h  Swimming classes 7–9 pm

## Holiday activities

**2** What can you do on these holidays? Complete the table with the activities. Some activities can go in more than one section.

> buy souvenirs   enjoy nature   go sightseeing
> go snorkelling   make a fire   see animals
> sleep in a tent   sunbathe

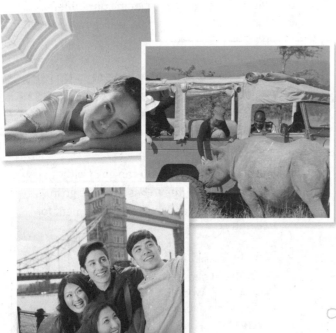

| wildlife holiday |
| --- |
|  |
| camping trip |
|  |
| city break |
|  |
| beach holiday |
|  |

## journey, travel and trip

**3** Choose the correct option in *italics*.

1 The *travel / journey / trip* from Paris to London only took two and a half hours.

2 Max is going on a *travel / journey / trip* to the mountains with his friends this Saturday.

3 How often do you *travel / journey / trip* abroad for work?

4 Train *travel / journey / trip* is the most popular way to get around the country.

5 I hope you have a good *travel / journey / trip* tonight and arrive safely.

6 Erin has to go on a lots of business *travels / journeys / trips* for her job.

### Listening Part 3

- Use the headings in the notes to help you follow the recording.

- You only need to write one or two words. At the end, check you haven't written more. Check if the words should be singular or plural.

**Exam advice**

**1**  For each question, write the correct answer in the gap. Write one or two words or a number or a date or a time.

You will hear a guide talking about tours of a film studio.

## OAKWOOD FILM STUDIOS

**Robert the Bruce tour**
The tour takes **(1)** .......................... .
Listen to **(2)** .......................... in a documentary you'll see about the film.

**The Totem Men tour**
This tour takes 30 minutes.
Visit **(3)** .......................... in the camp to learn about the daily life of Native Americans.

**Ricky Ranger tour**
This tour takes 45 minutes.
Learn how they made the
**(4)** .......................... for the film.

**Oakwood cafeteria and shop**
Our café sells great salads, burgers and pizzas.
It's closed on **(5)** .......................... .
You can buy souvenirs, such as **(6)** .......................... , in the shop before you leave.

## Writing Part 1

**Exam advice**

- Connect your ideas using linking words, e.g. *since, as* and *although*.
- Try to use interesting vocabulary. Don't repeat words like *good* or *nice*.

**1** Look at the exam task. Then tick (✓) the information (1–7) that the answer should include.

> Read this email, from your English-speaking friend Toni, and the notes you have made.
>
> Write your **email** to Toni, using **all the notes**.

**To:**

**From:** Toni

Hi,

Thanks for your letter. I wanted to tell you about my plans this summer. Jamie and I are going on holiday to your country in August. I'm really excited!    *Great!*

We'd like to visit some interesting places. Do you know a good place to go?    *Yes – say where it is*

What is the place like?    *Describe it*

We like sightseeing and being active. What can we do there that is fun?    *Recommend ...*

Write soon,

Toni

1  a comment about Toni's news ☐
2  the name and location of a place ☐
3  information about your last holiday ☐
4  a description of the place ☐
5  an invitation to visit someone's home ☐
6  a suggestion about an activity for a couple to do together ☐
7  a suitable opening and ending ☐

**2** Complete Talia's answer with the adjectives from the box. There may be more than one possibility.

> amazing   clean   delicious   excellent   fascinating   historic   long   pretty   warm

Dear Toni,

I'm really happy you're visiting my country.

I think the best place to go is a village called L'Escala. It's on the coast near Girona, which is very close to the border between France and Spain. The village is very **(1)** .......................... and the coast is absolutely **(2)** .......................... . There are lots of **(3)** .......................... restaurants and the food is **(4)** .......................... .

You can go snorkelling there because the water is extremely **(5)** .......................... , and there is a **(6)** .......................... beach where you can walk for hours. If you want to go sightseeing, there are some **(7)** .......................... places to visit or you can go shopping in the market on Sundays.

I hope you have a good holiday!

Love,

Talia

**3** Exam candidates often make mistakes with adjectives. Underline the mistakes in the sentences and correct them.

1  When we arrived at the top of the mountain we were absolutely tired.
2  We saw some fasinating sights on holiday.
3  It was amazed – the best experience of my life!
4  It's a very nice city with lots of historical buildings.
5  There was a beatiful view from the hotel balcony.
6  The rooms were a bit tiny, but the food was delicious.

**4** Write your own answer to the task from Exercise 1 in about 100 words. Use interesting adjectives.

# 5 Different feelings

**1** Choose the correct option in *italics*.

1 The team was *cheerful / disappointed* when they lost the match by one point.

2 I was *jealous / embarrassed* when my colleague got a bonus, but I didn't.

3 Isabelle never pays for anything when we go out, not even a coffee! She's so *serious / mean*.

4 Callum always sleeps with the light on, otherwise he feels *afraid / miserable* that something bad will happen.

5 I felt so *embarrassed / strange* when I forgot the words I had to say in the play.

6 I'm very *fond / bored* of Lily. She's so kind.

7 It was the first time I had to speak in public, so I was feeling *confident / nervous*.

8 Ethan felt *satisfied / ashamed* when his friend discovered he was lying.

**2** Complete the sentences with an adjective from the box and a preposition. Sometimes more than one answer is possible.

> afraid   angry   ashamed   bored   crazy
> depressed   pleased   sure

1 Poppy was ........................ ............... her sister when she borrowed her best dress without asking.

2 My cousin is ........................ ............... spiders and runs away when he sees one.

3 We were ........................ ............... watching TV all afternoon, so we turned it off and went out for a walk.

4 You should be ........................ ............... your behaviour. It's terrible to upset someone like that!

5 Charlie was ........................ ............... the painting he bought. It looks great.

6 He doesn't want to get out of bed in the morning because he's feeling ........................ ............... losing his job. I think he needs to see a doctor.

7 Are you ........................ ............... the time the train leaves? Just check it again.

8 Jake is ........................ ............... reggae music and listens to it all the time.

## Adjectives and their opposites

**3** Replace the adjectives in bold with an adjective from the box with the opposite meaning.

> complicated   fantastic   funny   generous
> miserable   ordinary   positive   relaxed

1 My brother is very **mean**. He always lets me borrow his things if I need them.

2 I was feeling **cheerful** because I missed the party and I really wanted to go.

3 Josh was so **serious** that I couldn't stop laughing.

4 Jessie's instructions were so **simple** that I couldn't do the activity.

5 The film was absolutely **awful**. I can't wait to see it again!

6 I love Lucy – she has such a **negative** attitude to life. Even when things go wrong, she manages to keep smiling.

7 Lydia is feeling **nervous** now that she's on holiday.

8 It was a very **strange** day because I got up, went to work, came home and went to bed, as usual.

## Adjectives with -ed and -ing

**4** Complete the sentences with the correct form of the words in brackets.

**1** (bore)
  **a** The long train journey was ............................
  **b** Sean was ........................... because he had nothing to do.

**2** (embarrass)
  **a** It was really ........................... when I fell over in the street.
  **b** I felt ........................... because I wore the wrong clothes to the party.

**3** (relax)
  **a** Sitting on the beach with a good book is ........................... .
  **b** I feel ........................... when I listen to music.

**4** (excite)
  **a** The friends are ........................... about the skiing trip.
  **b** The action film was really ........................... .

**5** (amuse)
  **a** Rachel laughed because the video clip was very ........................... .
  **b** My grandfather was ........................... when he heard the joke.

## Reading Part 4

**Exam advice**

- Decide which sentences are definitely wrong and then try to find evidence that shows why one of the remaining ones is right.
- Think about the grammar of the sentence. Do the pronouns in the options match the sentences before and after the gap – singular/plural, male/female, etc?

**1** Read the text about going to learn a language abroad. Did the writer enjoy the experience?

**2** Five sentences have been removed from the text. For each question, choose the correct answer. There are three extra sentences which you do not need to use.

Learning French in FRANCE

Finally the big day arrived. I was going to spend four months in France, learning French. I was feeling nervous and excited because this was my first time on a plane. **(1)** ............... We arrived at the airport, a couple of hours before the flight.

The flight was fine, although it was strange seeing the city disappearing under me from so high up. The flight went by quickly because I was so busy chatting to Alice about our trip and how different French life might be from life back home. During the flight, we decided that we shouldn't spend too much time together. **(2)** ............... Despite our agreement, I was worried that I wouldn't be able to say much the whole time I was in France. However, when my host family met me, I knew from the mother's warm smile that everything would be OK.

It was still a bit stressful at first, trying to understand and communicate, but after a couple of weeks it became easier. I spent a lot of time with a lovely young woman who was a friend of the family. **(3)** ............... In fact, I learnt loads of interesting words from her; you know, the kind of things you don't find in books! I had one embarrassing moment when I used the wrong word when I was talking to a waitress, but she was very relaxed about it. **(4)** ...............

When the time came to say goodbye to my host family, I was very sad to leave. However, I have brought back some wonderful memories from this experience. The most important thing I've learnt is that if you're open and positive about learning a language, then it's much easier. **(5)** ............... I've even started watching a television series in French and I'm surprised to find that I can understand a lot more than before my stay in France.

**A** I think she knew you can't expect a language student to get everything right!

**B** I've come back relaxed and much more confident in my ability.

**C** I've paid attention to them and worked hard to do well.

**D** We knew we wouldn't learn as much French if we did that.

**E** I found it disappointing when I didn't understand.

**F** She didn't have time to show me much.

**G** Luckily, Alice, my sister, was going as well.

**H** She was a bit younger than me, but we got on well.

# 5

## Grammar

### can, could, might and may

**1** Choose the correct option in *italics*.

1 When my grandad was younger he *can / could* see very well, but now he's old, he *can't / couldn't* read without glasses.

2 I'm not sure if I *can / may* finish this work today. I *can / might* have to do it tomorrow.

3 **A:** Where's Katie? I *can't / couldn't* find her.

   **B:** She *can / might* be in the canteen. I saw her going in that direction a few minutes ago.

4 The football match *can / may* be cancelled because it *might not / might* snow this weekend.

5 **A:** *Can / May* you play the piano?

   **B:** No, but my brother *can / might* play very well.

### Modals for advice, obligation and prohibition

**2** Choose the correct option in *italics*.

1 You *shouldn't / don't have to* go to bed late when you have to get up early the next day.

2 You *mustn't / have to* lie to people if you want to stay friends with them.

3 You *shouldn't / have to* pay if you break something in the shop.

4 You *ought to / shouldn't* eat vegetables every day to be healthy.

5 You *should / don't have to* bring food for the trip. Lunch will be provided.

6 We *don't have to / must* turn off the lights when we're out, to save electricity.

## Listening Part 2

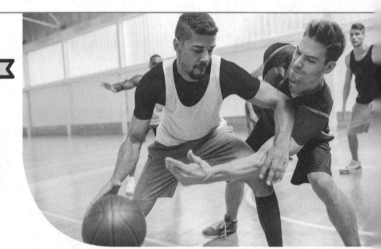

> • You will hear information related to all three options. The answer can be heard at the beginning, in the middle or at the end of the conversation. Don't tick the first thing you hear and then stop listening.
>
> • Check your answer the second time you hear the conversation.

**Exam advice**

**1** For each question, choose the correct answer.

**1** You will hear two friends talking about a basketball match.

The man is unhappy about the match because

 **A** his team didn't win.

 **B** it was boring.

 **C** the best player was injured.

**2** You will hear a woman talking to a friend about moving home.

How does she feel about it?

 **A** disappointed with the size of the house

 **B** pleased with the public transport in the area

 **C** worried about losing contact with her friends

**3** You will hear a student talking to a friend about a website.

He thinks it is good because

 **A** students can use the photos on the site.

 **B** it has all the information they need.

 **C** it's easy to use.

**4** You will hear two friends talking about a party.

The girl enjoyed the evening because

 **A** she got to know new people.

 **B** everyone was dancing.

 **C** she had an interesting conversation.

**5** You will hear a student telling a friend about a board game.

She found it boring because

 **A** the other players knew more about the game than she did.

 **B** she had to wait a long time for her turn.

 **C** no one wanted to talk while they were playing.

**6** You will hear two friends talking about a sports centre.

They agree that

 **A** the staff are welcoming.

 **B** the prices are reasonable.

 **C** it is well organised.

## Writing Part 2 (A story)

**Exam advice**

- Remember you should spend about 20 minutes writing your story. In this time, you need to plan the story, write it and check it.
- Try to use a variety of different words and adjectives.
- Don't write too many words over the limit – if you write too much, you are more likely to make mistakes.

**1** Read the exam question. The words and phrases in the box show ideas you could use in this story. Put them into the correct part of the table.

> Your English teacher has asked you to write a story. Your story must begin with this sentence.
>
> *I'll never forget the day everything went wrong.*

> angry   at work   miserable   on holiday   I lost something
> sad   my husband   nervous   a teacher
> a shop assistant   at home   I forgot something
> my family   depressed   I missed the bus/train
> a police officer   embarrassed   a friend
> disappointed   in a sports match
> I broke something   my wife

| Place(s) | |
| --- | --- |
| People | |
| Problem(s) | |
| Feelings | |

**2** Read the answer below and number the events A–E in order. Ignore the gaps in the story.

- A   The shower was cold.  ☐
- B   My shirt got dirty.  ☐
- C   I noticed I had the wrong shoes.  ☐
- D   I got the train.  ☐
- E   I went running.  ☑ 1

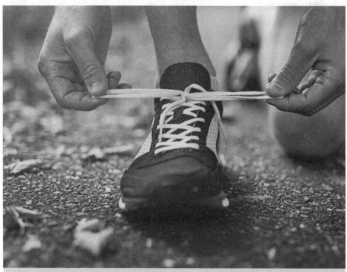

I'll never forget the day everything went wrong. It was a Friday. I was feeling excited and **(1)**............... because I had an important job interview that morning. I got up early, as usual, and went for a run, so that I would feel more relaxed. Afterwards, I got in the shower, but there was no hot water. Freezing cold, I got out quickly, put on my suit and tie and set off for the train.

The train was crowded, so I couldn't sit down. I was standing near the door when a woman got on with a takeaway coffee. The train moved suddenly and she spilt the coffee on my white shirt. I was really **(2)**.............. . Finally, when I got to the office for the interview the receptionist asked me to wait. I sat down, looked at my feet and realised that I was wearing trainers. I felt so **(3)**............... .

**3** Complete the story with an interesting adjective in each gap.

**4** Now answer this exam task.

> Your English teacher has asked you to write a story. Your story must begin with this sentence.
>
> *I remember the day I met my hero.*

Write your story in about 100 words. Think about the place, time, people and feelings. Try to use interesting adjectives.

# 6 That's entertainment!

## Vocabulary

### Television programmes

**1** Match the sentences with the types of television programme in the box.

> comedy series   cooking show   quiz show   reality show
> sports programme   the news   wildlife documentary

1 Challenge yourself to answer the questions.
2 24-hour information about world issues.
3 You won't stop laughing.
4 Follow the progress of future chefs.
5 You'll find out about every detail of their lives.
6 The exploration of our oceans and the creatures that live there.
7 All the Champions League matches live.

### Going out

**2** Complete the text with the words in the box.

> admission   book   interval   live   perform
> refreshments   screen   stage   subtitles
> tickets

### been/gone, meet, get to know, know and find out

**3** Choose the correct option in *italics*.

1 **A:** Have you *known* / *met* Michael for a long time?
  **B:** No, I only *knew* / *met* him last week.
2 **A:** What do you think of Lenny?
  **B:** I didn't like him at first, but now I've *got to know him* / *found him out* better, I think he's nice.
3 **A:** Where's Sean?
  **B:** I think he's *gone* / *been* home. He wasn't feeling well.
4 **A:** Hi Tom. Where have you *gone* / *been*? I wanted to ask you something.
  **B:** Sorry, I had to talk to my tutor in the break.
5 **A:** Have you ever *been* / *gone* to a live jazz concert?
  **B:** No, never, but I love watching rock bands.
6 **A:** Have you *found out* / *known* where we are going tomorrow?
  **B:** No, the tour guide hasn't told us yet.

Next week we have a complete range of events for all students at the university. On Wednesday evening there's a trip organised by the Music Club to see the Royal Opera Company **(1)** ............................................... at the National Opera House. There are limited places on the coach, so **(2)** ............................... early if you want to go. For film lovers, we are showing a series of short films from China on the big **(3)** ............................... in the Audio-visual department on Thursday night. The films will have **(4)** ............................... for those people who don't speak Chinese and **(5)** ............................... is free for all students with a student card. On Friday, our drama students will be on **(6)** ............................... in the Drama Club's performance of *Romeo and Juliet*. **(7)** ............................... will be provided in the **(8)** ............................... in the student café next to the main hall. And for fans of **(9)** ............................... music, join us for a special guitar concert in the café. You can get **(10)** ............................... for this event from the student events office on the first floor.

## Reading Part 2

# Saturday NIGHT — TV GUIDE

**1** The people below all want to watch TV tonight. Read the eight descriptions of TV programmes. Decide which programme would be the most suitable for each person.

**1** Musa is spending the evening with friends from his sports club. They want to learn something useful and see a programme with plenty of action.

**2** Sam would like to be a famous rock star one day. He loves listening to music from abroad and hearing new bands that aren't so famous. He isn't keen on competitions.

**3** Aisha wants to watch a competition, but she's bored with celebrities. She'd prefer to see something where normal people can take part.

**4** Paveen is looking after her eight-year-old cousin Maya, who is crazy about animals. They both want to watch something funny, and Maya's parents like her to watch educational programmes.

**5** Danny loves watching series, and he'd like to watch something that hasn't been on television before. He especially enjoys science-fiction shows that have famous actors in them.

**A Celebrity Challenge**

This great quiz show includes celebrity competitors who try to answer questions. Although these famous people come from the world of music or theatre, the questions are on any topic such as art, sport or history. Test yourself as you watch. All you have to do is download the app and if you beat the rest, there are fantastic prizes.

**B The Colony**

Switch on to the first part of this exciting new thriller. It is set in a galaxy far away where humans who escaped the destruction of Earth are now living. They learn to live with the aliens and deal with dangerous wildlife. It stars Oscar-winning actress, Tania Green. If you are interested in future worlds, this is one to watch.

**C Sunny**

This brand-new cartoon series follows the adventures of a group of penguins who play ice hockey. This sport takes them around the world to compete, and each week there is an original song performed by the polar bear fans. An amusing series that helps children learn about other cultures in an entertaining way, but older watchers will also enjoy it.

**D Reporter Jack**

This week Jack travels to the north of the country to meet a group of athletes training for the next World Games. They explain new training techniques for young people who want to succeed in field or track events. You can also see the most exciting moments in recent races.

**E Star Time**

The most popular weekly talent show on TV is now in its third season. Will a singer, a dancer or a gymnast win this week? From 6 to 60 years old, the performers have three minutes to give their best. They have often travelled from other countries to take part in the show.

**F Universe**

If you are a technology lover, then don't miss this special programme. We are all slightly scared about how much robots can control our lives, but here you will learn how they work and how we can control them. You can send a message to the experts and get instant on-screen answers.

**G Saturday Escape**

Imagine yourself skiing down a snowy mountain or parachuting from a plane. Well-known TV journalist Tiger Tom accepts a new challenge each week. This time it's bungee-jumping, and you can experience the jump moment by moment as he has a mini-camera attached to his helmet. Meanwhile his commentary about the experience will keep you laughing even though it's scary.

**H Show Night Special**

Continuing our events series, this week's programme brings you a live concert held to celebrate World Music Day. Some well-known stars, as well as bands you've never seen before, will come together on stage. Musicians from over 30 countries will perform, and between songs they give tips on how to begin a career in music.

# 6

## Grammar
### Present perfect and past simple

**1** Complete the sentences with words from the box.

> already   for   just   since   yet

1 Oscar's been a successful actor ............................ six years.
2 I have to give the project in next week, but I'm relaxed because I've ............................ done it.
3 The film has ............................ finished, so you can turn on your phone now.
4 She hasn't seen her uncle ............................ she was a child.
5 I haven't had any information about the exhibition ............................ . I hope they'll send it tomorrow.
6 You don't need to call Danny. I've ............................ told him what time we have to be there.
7 Lorena's ............................ gone out. She left two minutes ago.
8 Have you received my email ............................ ? The internet is so slow today.

**2** Complete the sentence with the correct tense of the verb in brackets. Use the past simple or present perfect.

1 How long ............................ (you / know) your best friend?
2 I ............................ (take) hundreds of photos on my last holiday.
3 I ............................ (not be) to the new stadium yet, but I want to go next week.
4 He ............................ (learn) to ride a bike when he was four.
5 I ............................ (tell) you three times already. Don't touch my computer!
6 We ............................ (go) to see a brilliant play last week.

**3** Exam candidates often make mistakes with the present perfect and past simple.
Underline and correct one mistake in each sentence.

1 I have had fun last weekend with my friends.
   ....................................................................

2 He's bought the tickets yet.
   ....................................................................

3 Have you ever gone to Italy on holiday?
   ....................................................................

4 We are friends since I was six years old.
   ....................................................................

5 I know him for about ten years.
   ....................................................................

6 They already seen the film.
   ....................................................................

## Listening Part 1

> • You will hear information about all three pictures. Listen to the complete conversation before you choose your answer.
> **Exam advice**

**1** For each question, choose the correct answer.

07 **1** Which programme did the man enjoy?

A    B    C

**2** How much did the ticket cost?

A    B    C

**3** Where does the woman want to watch the football match?

A    B    C

**4** Which shirt does the man buy?

A    B    C

**5** Who is the man's tennis coach?

**A**         **B**         **C**

**6** What has the girl forgotten?

**A**         **B**         **C**

**7** When did the concert finish?

**A**         **B**         **C**

## Writing Part 2 (An article)

> **Exam advice**
> - Read the task and make notes to answer the questions. Use examples to explain your ideas and give your opinion.
> - Use different paragraphs to write about each question.

**1** You can use a question in an article to attract the reader's attention. Put the words in order to make questions.

**1** ever / basketball / seen / Have / a / live / you / match / ?

.................................................................................

.................................................................................

**2** people / Why / do / like / weekend / cinema / to / the / at / going / the / ?

.................................................................................

.................................................................................

**3** you / going / Do / out / home / prefer / or / night / staying / Saturday / on / at / a / ?

.................................................................................

.................................................................................

**2** Match the sentences A–C to the questions in Exercise 1.

**A** I enjoy both. It depends on how I feel.

**B** I think they enjoy the experience of seeing a film on the big screen.

**C** I went to the European Cup final and it was an amazing experience.

**3** Read this exam task and the student's article below. Answer the questions.

**1** What two forms of entertainment does the writer choose to write about?

**2** What examples does the writer give?

**3** What does the writer use to attract the reader's attention?

> You see this announcement in an international English-language magazine.
>
> **Articles wanted!**
>
> **SATURDAY NIGHT ENTERTAINMENT**
> What's a good way to spend Saturday night?
> Music? Film? TV shows? Sport?
> Is it better to watch films at home or at the cinema? Why?
> Write an article answering these questions and we will publish the most interesting articles in our magazine.
>
> Write your article.

> Is anything better than spending Saturday night with family or friends? My wife and I often sit down together to watch a comedy show. We usually have dinner and then turn on the TV. I love it because the next day is Sunday, so I don't have to worry about getting up for work.
>
> Sometimes we like going out to the cinema, too. It's fantastic to see a good film on a big screen. The sound is better and you can feel you are part of the action.
>
> If we want to have a special evening, we prefer to go to the cinema and maybe have dinner afterwards.

**4** Write your own answer to the task in Exercise 3 in about 100 words. Try to include a question, an example and mention at least two of the types of entertainment given in the question.

# 7 Getting around

## Reading Part 1

> **Exam advice**
> • Don't try to match words in the options with words in the text. Think about their meaning rather than the actual words.
> • Check that the meaning of the option you think is the correct answer exactly matches the information in the text.

**1** For each question, choose the correct answer.

**1**

> Hi Toni, I missed the train, so I'll be a bit late. I know you haven't got much time, so just go on to the restaurant and order lunch – I'll have an omelette and salad! Rob

**A** Rob wants Toni to go to eat alone.
**B** Rob is reminding Toni that she needs to hurry.
**C** Rob is telling Toni to get some food for him.

**2**

> **CUSTOMERS' CAR PARK NEXT TO THE SUPERMARKET**
>
> **TWO HOURS FREE PARKING.**
> **30€ IF YOU STAY OVER THIS TIME.**

**A** Customers must pay if their shopping takes more than two hours.
**B** Customers can park free only if they spend 30€ in the supermarket.
**C** Customers can't park longer than two hours.

**3**

> **To:** Olivia
> **From:** Ali
>
> I'm sorry to hear about your broken arm. Our last match wasn't great. We needed you – you're our strongest player! Next week we're going to play at home. Come and see us!

Why has Ali sent Olivia this message?
**A** to see if Olivia will play with them next week
**B** to let Olivia know that she is important for her team
**C** to check if Olivia injured herself doing sport

**4**

> **Tennis court booking**
> Due to routine software changes our online booking service will be suspended on Friday from 7 pm to 8 am the following day. Apologies to our members for the inconvenience.

**A** Customers won't be able to make a reservation by computer after 7 pm on Friday.
**B** The website will be out of service because of unexpected technical problems.
**C** If you can't access the service, you should install new software.

**5**

> Alice
> To get to my house, take the 27 bus. When you get off the train, the stop's opposite the main entrance to the station. Then it's five stops away. I'm on the corner of Beech Street.
> Oscar

**A** Alice needs to take a bus to the station.
**B** Alice should get on the bus on the corner.
**C** Alice should count the stops to find Oscar's house.

## Vocabulary
### Weather

**1** Complete the sentences with the words in the box.

> foggy  freezing  frost  ice  rainy  showers
> snowy  sunshine  thunderstorms  windy

1 It's white outside this morning, but it hasn't snowed. There's ............................ on the grass.

2 The rain started and stopped several times today. There were several ............................ .

3 It was like driving through a cloud, so we had to go really slowly. It was very ............................ .

4 It was so cold that the lake was frozen. You could see the fish under the ............................ .

5 The temperature is below zero. It's ............................ .

6 When there are ............................ my dog is terrified by the noise and won't leave the house.

7 Take an umbrella in the ............................ season in Thailand because it can be very wet.

8 The main reason my sister goes on holiday to the beach is to enjoy the ............................ .

9 It's often very ............................ in that area near the sea, so it's popular with kite surfers.

10 I love it when the weather is ............................ and cold in the winter because we usually go skiing.

**2** Exam candidates often make spelling mistakes. Underline the mistakes in the sentences and correct them.

1 The weather was suny and there weren't any clouds in the sky. ............................

2 The temperture was about 30 degrees all week! ............................

3 There was a terrible thuderstorm that lasted for ages. ............................

4 During the day it's very hot, but at night it's frezzing. ............................

5 The wheather was great on Saturday, so we went to the beach. ............................

6 It was rainning a lot, so I took my umbrella with me. ............................

7 In the fogy weather the plane couldn't take off. ............................

8 The tree was struck by lightening during the storm. ............................

## Compound words

**3** Match the words in box A with the words in box B to make compound words. Then complete the sentences.

A

> back  camp  cross  guide  over  sight  sign  suit

B

> book  cases  night  pack  post  roads  seeing  site

1 There is a ............................ at the ............................ showing the way.

2 The people want to do some ............................ , so they've got a ............................ to find the best places, but first they should leave their ............................ at the hotel!

3 We stayed ............................ at a ............................ . I had to carry everything in my ............................ .

**7**

## Listening Part 4

1 · 08 **For each question, choose the correct answer.**

**You will hear an interview with a student called Adam, who is going on a trip to the desert this summer.**

1 Adam is going to the desert to
   A see how people live.
   B plan a building project.
   C help in a medical centre.

2 Adam hopes to
   A record most of the journey with his camera.
   B get more support for the project.
   C reach the camp quickly.

3 What does Adam say about the digital camera?
   A He can only use it for a limited time.
   B He has to borrow it from someone.
   C He uses it more at the end of the day.

4 What difficulty might Adam have?
   A having enough clothes
   B staying warm at night
   C keeping cool during the day

5 Adam will eat food that is
   A brought from a different place.
   B provided by the local people.
   C unique to the desert.

6 Adam is anxious because
   A he doesn't know how to communicate with the local people.
   B he might not sleep well.
   C he hasn't travelled to a foreign country before.

## Grammar
### *too* and *enough*

1 **Complete the second sentence so that it means the same as the first. Use *too* or *enough*.**

1 I couldn't eat the soup. It was really hot.
   The soup was ................................................. to eat.

2 She's only 16 years old. She can't get married.
   She isn't ................................................. to get married.

3 My house is far from the town centre. I can't walk there.
   My house is ................................................. from the town centre to walk there.

4 He's very clever. He can go to a good university.
   He's ................................................. to go to a good university.

5 It was very dark. They couldn't see the road.
   It was ................................................. to see the road.

6 My jacket isn't warm. I can't wear it for skiing.
   My jacket isn't ................................................. to wear it for skiing.

7 I've only got two seats in my car. I can't take both of you to the station.
   My car is ................................................. to take both of you to the station.

8 There are a lot of people. We can't give them all free tickets.
   There are ................................................. people to give them all free tickets.

### *extremely, fairly, quite, rather, really* and *very*

2 **Choose the correct option in *italics*.**

1 The play was *extremely / fairly* interesting, but I thought the second half was a little boring.

2 She worked *really / quite* hard and got a promotion after a year.

3 I'm *rather / quite* sure that Ollie's at home now, so let's go and see him.

4 I'm *really / fairly* surprised they went to see that film – they hate romantic comedies.

## Prepositions of movement

**3** Choose the correct option in *italics*.

1 The detective jumped *into / onto* his car and drove away quickly.
2 She fell as she was getting *off / out of* the taxi and hurt her knee.
3 Have you ever been on a long journey *by / on* ship?
4 Your plane got here *at / on* time, so I didn't have to wait.
5 You should always get *up / on* a horse on the left-hand side.
6 Get *off / out of* the bus at the stop after the museum.

## The future

**4** Choose the correct option in *italics*.

1 I've just bought a new video game. *I'll bring / I bring* it with me this afternoon.

2 The match *starts / is starting* at 10 am. Don't be late!

3 I can't see you this afternoon. *I'm playing / I'll play* basketball.

4 My sister *will get / is going to get* married next April.

5 When *does your train arrive / is your train arriving*? I can meet you at the station.

6 Thanks for the invitation! *I'll see / I'm going to see* you tomorrow.

**5** Complete the dialogues with the verb in brackets. Use *will* or *going to*.

1 A: Why are you putting on your coat?
   B: I ........................ (see) a friend.
2 A: I'm really thirsty.
   B: I ........................ (get) you some water.
3 A: What are your plans for this weekend?
   B: I ........................ (visit) my aunt.
4 A: I can't find my wallet.
   B: Don't worry. I ........................ (help) you look for it.
5 A: Did you phone Alex?
   B: Oh, I forgot. I ........................ (call) her now.
6 A: What do you want to eat, pizza or pasta?
   B: I ........................ (have) pizza, please.

## Writing Part 1

**Exam advice**

- When you finish writing, check your work, especially the verb tenses, spelling and prepositions.
- If you want to change something, cross out the word and write the correct word clearly above it.

**1** Look at the exam task and the student's answer below. Correct the <u>underlined</u> mistakes.

> Read this email from your English-speaking friend Alex and the notes you have made.

**To:**
**From:** Alex
Hi,

How's it going? You know it's Lucy's birthday soon. Shall we organise a surprise for her? I thought maybe a meal in a restaurant or a party at my house. Which would be better?

*I forgot!*

*Tell Alex*

Next weekend might be good, will you be free then?

*Yes – say when*

What can we get her as a present? I know she likes clothes.

*Suggest . . .*

Let me know what you think!
Lots of love,
Alex

Write your email to Alex, using all the notes.

Hi Alex,
I didn't remember Lucy's birthday! We must do something to celebrate. Both your ideas are great, but I'd like to go **(1)** <u>at</u> a restaurant. I expect it'll be **(2)** <u>suny</u> next weekend, so we can eat outside in that place in the square. Next Saturday, I'm going to see my parents **(3)** <u>to</u> lunch, but Sunday is perfect.
Why don't we buy Lucy some **(4)** <u>sunglass</u>? They **(5)** <u>are</u> useful for the celebration on Sunday and for the rest of the summer. I **(6)** <u>have seen</u> some really nice ones **(7)** <u>on</u> a shop yesterday. Is that a good idea? If you agree, I **(8)** <u>buy</u> them on my way home from work.
Bye for now,
Ryan

**2** Write your own answer to the task in Exercise 1 in about 100 words. Check your work when you have finished.

# 8 Influencers

## Vocabulary
### Phrasal verbs

**1** Complete the text with the correct form of the phrasal verbs in the box.

> bring up   find out   get on   grow up   make up
> run out of   set up   take up

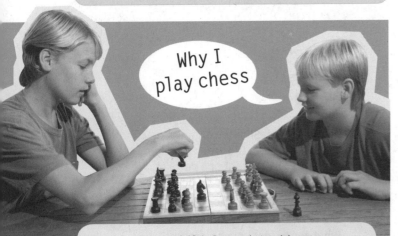

Why I play chess

When I was a child I used to **(1)** ............................ stories all the time, and I wanted to become a famous writer. Now, I'm not famous, but I am a writer! My parents were quite strict. They **(2)** ............................ my brother and me without any electronics or TV, so we **(3)** ............................ with books and games. We used to start a chess game at the beginning of the week and we tried to finish it by the weekend. Sometimes we **(4)** ............................ time, so we continued playing on Sunday. My brother and I generally **(5)** ............................ well with each other except when one of us **(6)** ............................ that the other had moved a chess piece in secret.

I still play now that I'm an adult. Last year, I even **(7)** ............................ electronic chess, although playing against the computer isn't as much fun as playing with my brother. This year I'm planning to **(8)** ............................ a chess club in the village where I live.

## Describing people

**2** Correct the adjective in bold with an adjective that means the opposite. You are given the first letter.

1 The history professor is very **easy-going** and doesn't let us in his lectures if we are late. s............................
2 John is very **hard-working** and spends a lot of time on the sofa watching TV. l............................
3 Tamara's so **stupid**. I'm sure she'll get a good job in the future. c............................
4 The street was **noisy** because there was no traffic. q............................
5 My brother gave me a new phone for my birthday. He's so **mean**. g............................
6 Don't push in front of other people, Jack! It's **polite**. r............................
7 They felt **calm** as they were waiting for news of the election. a............................
8 She's very **shy** and loves talking in public. c............................

**3** Complete the sentences with an adjective formed from the word in brackets.

1 My best friend always seems ............................, even when things aren't going well. (cheer)
2 The train service here is ............................. The trains are always late. (reliable)
3 Human babies are ............................ for much longer than most animals. (help)
4 She looks ............................ in that long dress. (beauty)
5 The weather was so ............................ that we had to cancel the barbecue. (pleasant)
6 He's always telling lies. He's completely ............................. (honest)
7 The book became a ............................ film and it won an Oscar. (success)
8 I found your instructions very ............................ and managed to set up the computer by myself. (help)
9 Marc gets angry quickly if he has to wait. He's so ............................. (patient)
10 Lizzie won't talk to me. I don't know why she's so ............................. (friendly)

# 8

**4** Complete the sentences with a word from the box.

> bald  beard  blonde  broad  curly  dark  grey
> long  moustache  pale  short  straight  wavy

**1** She's got ........................... , ........................... , ........................... hair.

**2** He's got ........................... , ........................... , brown hair and ........................... shoulders.

**3** She's got long, ........................... hair and ........................... skin.

**4** He's got long, ........................... , ........................... hair and a ........................... .

**5** He's ........................... and he's got a black ........................... .

## Reading Part 6

**Exam advice**

- First, read the whole text quickly to get an idea of what it is about.
- If you think there are a few possible answers, read the whole sentence, try each word and decide which fits best. Very occasionally, there may be more than one possible answer, but you must only write one answer for each gap.

**1** For each question, write the correct answer. Write *one* word in each gap.

# Influences

When we decide to buy a particular product or take up a particular activity, we usually think we are making an independent decision. Often, we don't realise **(1)** ........................... much we are influenced by the people around us and the messages we receive.

One influence is clearly our family. **(2)** ........................... your parents are interested in travelling, for example, then you probably will be, too. Or sometimes we like to show we are different from others, so we choose a sport or a hobby that no one in our family **(3)** ........................... done before.

Friends' attitudes and opinions affect us, too. We often want to be like **(4)** ........................... , so sometimes we copy what they do. Advertising also influences us more **(5)** ........................... we think. Frequent messages about a particular food or drink, with images of young people having fun, make us think that we should **(6)** ........................... least try it.

**8**

## Grammar

### Zero, first and second conditionals

**1** Complete the sentences with the correct form of the verb in brackets to make zero, first and second conditionals. Write 0, 1 or 2 next to the sentence.

1 Jemma will be pleased if she ........................ (get) that job. ............
2 I ........................ (tell) my parents if I had a problem. ............
3 Next week, I'll be in Paris if my plans ........................ (go) well. ............
4 ........................ (you / travel) by plane if you had enough money? ............
5 If you ask my cousin, he ........................ (give) you some good advice. ............
6 If Tom ........................ (wake up) late, he doesn't usually have breakfast. ............
7 If they were smarter, they ........................ (not do) such stupid things. ............
8 If I ........................ (find) a good video on the internet, I send the link to my friends. ............

### when, if and unless

**2** Complete the sentences with *when, if* or *unless*.

1 I've lost my phone. ........................ anyone finds it, please put it on my desk.
2 I wouldn't have a dog as a pet ........................ I had a garden.
3 I'd sleep all morning on Saturday ........................ I didn't have an interview at 9 o'clock.
4 Lucas always checks his blog ........................ he gets up in the morning.
5 She'll be worried about you ........................ you phone her to say where you are.
6 We set up the YouTube channel ........................ we started selling our products.
7 I'd like to be a volunteer ........................ I leave university.
8 You won't become famous ........................ a lot of people see your videos.

**3** Match the beginnings and endings of the sentences and complete them with *if, when* or *unless*.

1 I'll wait for you in the café
2 I don't usually lend money to friends
3 It's hard to speak in front of a lot of people
4 We only follow famous people online
5 He'll need to check in
6 We'll be happy to see you
7 You shouldn't put their photos on your blog
8 I won't buy those trousers

a ............ they give their permission.
b ............ he gets to the airport.
c ............ they give interesting advice.
d ............ you're very confident.
e ............ you come to London next week.
f ............ it's an emergency.
g ............ your train is late.
h ............ the price is reduced.

**4** Exam candidates often make mistakes with conditionals.
Underline and correct one vocabulary mistake in each sentence.

1 If you came, can you bring something to eat or drink?
2 Did you join a gym if you wanted to get fit?
3 Unless he has got time, he'll come to see you.
4 If Anna doesn't have to work, she'd go travelling more.
5 My friend will be delighted if she won the competition.
6 When you are going to the picnic, you can bring some food.

## Listening Part 3

**1** For each question, write the correct answer in the gap. Write *one* or *two words* or a *number* or a *date* or a *time*.

You will hear a lecturer talking to a group of students about a young couple who have set up a fruit juice business.

# Get Wonky fruit juice

Maciek and Karina set up their business in (1) ............................ .

They use fruit that can't be sold to shops because it is the wrong (2) ............................ and size.

The fruit juice they make does not contain (3) ............................ .

To begin with, they used (4) ............................ as containers for the juice.

They have borrowed £ (5) ............................ to help build their business.

They are planning to sell their juices to (6) ............................ .

## Writing Part 2 (An article)

**1** Read this exam task and the student's article below. Find five spelling mistakes and five punctuation mistakes.

You see this notice in an international English-language magazine for teenagers.

> **Articles wanted!**
>
> **WHAT MAKES A GOOD FRIEND?**
> What kind of character should a good friend have?
> Should a good friend have the same hobbies and opinions as you? Why?
>
> **Write an article answering these questions and we will publish the best ones.**

Write your **article**.

A good friend is a kind person who always listens to you. You dont need to have a lot of similar interests.

One of my best friends is Hassan. I don't ofen see him because he's gone to study in england, but we have funn when we see each other in the holiday's. He's studying Fisics but I'm doing Fine Arts. Although we have different habilities we complement each other.

Hes a very calm person. I think that's the perfect character for a good freind because he's easy to be with.

**2** Write your own answer to the task in Exercise 1 in about 100 words. Check your spelling and punctuation.

# 9 Stay fit and healthy

Listening Part 2

**Exam advice**

- Don't worry if you don't understand everything. You only need to understand the parts of the recording that answer the questions.

- The words you hear will not always be the same as in the question. Think about different words that can mean the same.

**1** For each question, choose the correct answer.

**1** You will hear a man talking to a friend about their exercise class.
Why did he miss the class last week?

**A** Someone needed his help.

**B** He wasn't well.

**C** His car broke down.

**2** You will hear two friends talking about a table tennis competition.
What does the man say about it?

**A** It will be an opportunity to meet new people.

**B** It will be a change from his routine.

**C** It will be important that they win.

**3** You will hear a woman telling her friend about a football match she went to.
She was disappointed because

**A** someone's behaviour bothered her.

**B** the weather was terrible.

**C** her team played badly.

**4** You will hear two friends talking about a trip to an art gallery.
What do they agree about?

**A** how original the exhibition was

**B** how interesting a member of the staff was

**C** how well objects were displayed

**5** You will hear a boy talking to his mother.
Why was the young man unable to call her?

**A** He didn't have time to do it.

**B** His phone didn't work.

**C** He didn't have his phone with him.

**6** You will hear two friends talking about going skiing.
The girl tells the boy

**A** to expect to fall.

**B** to be careful of other skiers.

**C** to buy good equipment.

## Vocabulary
### Sports

**1** Choose the correct option in *italics* and write the name of the sport. Use the photos to help you.

**1** Arsenal *beat / won* Chelsea two goals to one in the match yesterday. ..............................

**2** Both athletes got the gold medal because they *drew / scored* in the final race. ..............................

**3** He used a *bat / helmet* to hit the ball. ..............................

**4** They wore thick *trainers / gloves* and heavy boots because of the cold. ..............................

**5** He broke his *bat / racket* when he fell on the wet court. ..............................

**6** The *track / score* was 24–25 to the other team when I hit the ball into the net, so we lost. ..............................

**2** Complete the text with the words from the box.

> bike   breath   exercise   exhausted   mountain biking
> rollerblading   skateboard   surfers

# WHEELS AND FITNESS

The invention of the wheel didn't only improve transport, but also produced many sporting activities. The two wheels on a **(1)** ............................ can take you much faster and further than your two feet. The inventor of **(2)** ............................ decided to put a line of wheels on his shoes.

Some people say the **(3)** ............................ was invented by **(4)** ............................ who wanted the same experience on land as on the sea, so they put wheels on small boards. Although wheels can help us move more easily, these forms of **(5)** ............................ still require a lot of energy. **(6)** ............................ up and down tracks in the countryside certainly keeps you fit, and skateboarding will leave you out of **(7)** ............................ as much as jogging. I tried rollerblading for the first time the other day, and after an hour, I was **(8)** ............................ !

### Illnesses and accidents

**3** Match the beginnings and endings of these sentences.

**1** If you have earache,
**2** When you have flu,
**3** If you sprain your ankle,
**4** When you cut yourself,
**5** Doctors will take an X-ray
**6** When you injure yourself,
**7** Doctors sometimes recommend a blood test
**8** You should keep your neck warm

**a** you sometimes get a bruise.
**b** take a pill, like an aspirin.
**c** you'll need to put a bandage on it.
**d** you usually have a high temperature.
**e** if you have a high fever.
**f** if you have a cough.
**g** put a plaster on.
**h** if they think you have fractured a bone.

## Reading Part 3

- Read the whole text first before you look at the questions.
- For each question, find the words in the text that tell you which option to choose.

**1** For each question, choose the correct answer.

# Katie Swan

Katie Swan was born in Bristol in 1999 and is one of the most promising young tennis players from the UK. Unlike many top players nowadays whose interest in the sport is decided for them when they are hardly able to hold a racket, she wasn't an early starter but began lessons at the age of seven. During her adolescence she didn't give up other activities for tennis; she also played competitive hockey and did well at school.

After a few years, she moved with her family to the USA. She went to a local school there, not because of the tennis opportunities, but because her father's job took her family there. She could also enjoy more hours of sunshine to play outdoors and her game quickly improved. She made a lot of friends, but she never lost her feeling of being British or her accent!

When she was 15, she was proud to reach number two in the world as a junior player, and then the following year, she played very well for the British team. However, doing a lot of sport and training so much can be hard on a player's body, and Katie suffered from back pain. When she was 17, she was upset because an injury to her foot meant that she couldn't finish the Wimbledon Junior tournament in London that year. Since then she has continued to compete internationally and managed to get through to the second round of the adult Wimbledon event in 2018 as well as playing in tournaments in Spain, Portugal and Brazil, among others.

Katie says the lifestyle of a professional tennis player is a challenge. It's not always easy being away from home and spending all your time in strange hotels. She loves competing, especially when she wins a match, which she does quite often. Katie has certainly become more confident by playing in international competitions, but she still feels nervous before an important match.

**1** What do we learn about Katie from the first paragraph?
- **A** She always knew she wanted to play tennis professionally.
- **B** Her first lessons were hard for her.
- **C** She began learning tennis later than most tennis stars do.
- **D** Her school work was more important than her tennis.

**2** She went to live in the USA because
- **A** she wanted to concentrate more on her tennis.
- **B** the weather was better for sporting activities.
- **C** she needed to go to a better school.
- **D** her father had to work there.

**3** What disappointment did she have in her late teens?
- **A** She didn't become number one among the junior players.
- **B** She didn't have time to train enough.
- **C** She couldn't win an important competition.
- **D** She didn't play in international competitions.

**4** What does she enjoy most about being a professional tennis player?
- **A** the experience of travelling to lots of different places
- **B** the pleasure of competition
- **C** the feeling she has when she is about to play
- **D** playing international matches

**5** What would be a good title for this article?
- **A** A star whose family gave up everything for her career
- **B** A great future for a player who never loses
- **C** Achieving a childhood ambition
- **D** Playing tennis through the good times and the bad

## Grammar

### Relative clauses

**1** Complete the sentences with the correct relative pronoun – *which, that, who, whose, when* or *where*.

1 This is the athlete ............................. won the 100m race.

2 The runner, ............................. trainers were old, couldn't run very well.

3 I first saw Ronaldo play in 2015, ............................. I went to the Cup Final.

4 Matt, ............................. was taking part in the bike race, was injured when he hit a rock.

5 It's the most famous court in the UK, ............................. the Wimbledon tennis final is played.

6 The local sports centre, ............................. was built in 1950, now needs to be repaired.

**2** Make one sentence from the pairs in 1–5, using a relative pronoun and making any other necessary changes.

1 There's the man. He lives in the flat next door.
There's the man .................................................................

2 That's the girl. Her mother was my nurse in hospital.
That's the girl .................................................................

3 2010 was the year. Our team won the cup.
2010 was the year .................................................................

4 This is the church. My parents got married here.
This is the church .................................................................

5 My only brother moved to Australia. He is a pilot.
My only brother, ............................................... , moved to Australia.

**3** Exam candidates often make mistakes with relative pronouns.

Underline and correct one vocabulary mistake in each sentence.

1 Those are the people which live in the house on the corner.

2 There are a lot of students use the library.

3 I remember the house where I used to live there.

4 The girl that we saw her on the bus is Jack's friend.

5 The man, who's passport was false, was arrested.

### Past perfect

**4** Complete the sentences with the verb in brackets in the past simple or past perfect.

1 Her granddad was feeling weak because he ............................. (have) an operation.

2 When we ............................. (finish) the match, we went out for a meal.

3 Why ............................. (you / go) home before the match had ended?

4 Jacob ............................. (see) the film, but he didn't mind seeing it again.

5 By the time she ............................. (get) to the restaurant, everyone had started eating.

6 Caitlin went to see the nurse because she ............................. (hurt) her leg.

## Writing Part 2 (A story)

- You can connect the sentences in the story with words like *then, next, finally,* etc.

- You can make the story more interesting by using words like *suddenly, luckily,* etc.

**Exam advice**

**1** Look at the exam task and complete the student's answer with the words from the box.

> Your English teacher has asked you to write a story. Your story must begin with this sentence.
> *I'll always remember the most important day of my life.*

| after   finally   luckily   suddenly   then   when |

I'll always remember the most important day of my life.

I got up early and I was ready to go **(1)** ............................. my friend knocked on the door. I said goodbye to my wife,

**(2)** ............................. we went to the city centre, where there were hundreds of people waiting to run the marathon.

**(3)** ............................., I already knew where I had to go to start. I felt prepared for the race. I began slowly, but **(4)** .............................

the first ten kilometres, I was already beginning to feel tired.

**(5)** ............................., I saw all my friends standing by the side of the road, waving. That gave me energy and **(6)** .............................

I reached the finish line. I had done my first marathon!

**2** Now answer this exam task.

> Your English teacher has asked you to write a story. Your story must begin with this sentence.
> *Sam was both anxious and excited when he left the house.*

Now write your **story** in about **100** words.

## Reading Part 2

**1** The people below all want to go shopping. Read the descriptions of eight shopping areas. Decide which shopping area would be the most suitable for each person.

**1** Jamila's going to a party tonight and wants to buy something new to wear, but she hasn't got much money. She also has to get a cake for the party.

**2** Chen's going to stay with friends abroad and wants to buy a present for their teenage son, who is into music. He wants something original and he hasn't got much space in his suitcase.

**3** Karen's working till 8 pm but she wants to buy a present, like a bracelet or a necklace, for a friend's birthday tomorrow. Karen wants something her friend can take back if she doesn't like it.

**4** Niran needs some new football boots. He's not sure what kind to buy, so he wants to try a variety of styles and wants someone to help him choose.

**5** Melanie wants to buy a good-quality garden chair that she'll be able to leave outside all year round. She'll have to take her car to bring it home.

# Where to shop guide:

### A Centre Place
This shopping centre has a number of shops specialising in outdoor activities. Don't miss the footwear stores, where you can get expert advice on a wide range of makes and models. You can also find camping goods, such as lightweight chairs and tables, and fishing equipment. Late-night closing on Fridays and Saturdays.

### B SMITH'S
All you could want for sports fans: 20,000 m² of clothes and equipment for athletes, hikers, team sport players, etc. Modern shopping means you simply choose what you want and pay at the automatic check-out. With no queuing, you'll be in and out in a moment. Open till 10 pm every day. Free parking for customers.

### C Holly Corner
This area of small expensive boutiques is a must for shoppers who love stylish clothes and classic gifts. The jewellery shops will offer you a personal service to help you decide on just the right item. Visit the Vintage Café for tea and a slice of delicious homemade cake after the shops close at 5 pm.

### D Newton Cross
A five-floor department store, famous for their wide range of gold and silver jewellery and good-quality clothes. Shopping here is easy because goods can be returned with no questions asked, although it can be more expensive than other shops in the area. Open 10 am – 10 pm every day. Car park on the lower levels.

**E** *Oak Lane*

This street market, held every day in the pedestrian zone, offers a variety of stalls selling small kitchen items and garden products, fresh food, and much more. You can find fashionable dresses, trousers and typical T-shirts printed with the faces of famous singers or sports stars at low prices. Don't miss the tasty products from Sam's Bakery. Open 8.00 to 15.00.

**F HIGHVIEW CENTRE**

Highview centre is located outside the city centre but has a large parking area for customers. This shopping centre offers all you could want for the home. They have a wide range of furniture suitable for both outdoor and indoor use, from cheap and cheerful plastic to stronger and more solid varieties that will last for years. Open every day except Sundays, 9.00–21.00.

**G north end**

An unusual mix of stalls in this market sell goods for music lovers, especially second-hand guitars and violins, locally grown plants and flowers, and organic foods such as cheese, meat and homemade jams. Parking can be difficult, so go early. Open from 8.00 to 15.00.

**H Satton Street**

A US-style shopping mall with fast-food restaurants, cheap doughnut cafés and electronics shops which will attract young people. You can find the latest in technology such as mini-headphones or fitness watches. Every week there are new devices that you've never seen before. Open till 8 pm.

*course, dish, food, meal* and *plate*

**1** Choose the correct option in *italics*.

1 Some people say the most important *food / meal* of the day is breakfast.
2 What time of day do they have their *main / large* meal in China?
3 In my country, we usually have three *plates / courses* at lunchtime.
4 The speciality in that restaurant is a spicy chicken *dish / meal*.
5 The best *meal / food* in the town is served in the Turkish restaurant.
6 What would you like for *starters / dessert*? Ice cream, chocolate mousse or fruit?
7 I have an allergy to dairy *produces / products*, so I don't drink cow's milk.
8 I'm playing in a match this afternoon, so I only want a *short / light* lunch.

**Shops and services**

**2** Complete the sentences with the name of a shop or service.

1 They went to the ............................ to borrow a book.
2 He took his car to the ............................ in the next town to have it repaired.
3 We went to the ............................ to get a loaf of bread.
4 Can you go to the ............................ to get some aspirin for me?
5 She bought the novel in the local ............................ .
6 I had my hair dyed at the ............................ last week.
7 My tooth is hurting, so I need to go to the ............................ .
8 You can't wash that leather jacket. You'll have to take it to the ............................ .

**3** Complete the sentences with a word in the box.

> book   borrow   buy
> complain   make

1 There's no need to buy a map. We can ............................ one from the library.
2 Will you phone the hotel to ............................ a room for tomorrow night?
3 If you want to see the doctor, you'll have to ............................ an appointment.
4 He lost his phone charger, so he had to ............................ another one.
5 The coach in the kick-boxing class was terrible. I'm going to ............................ to the sports centre.

## Grammar

### have something done

**1** Complete sentence B so that it means the same as sentence A. Use *have something done*.

**1 A** Someone cleans my car every Saturday.
  **B** I .................................................................... every Saturday.

**2 A** Did someone paint their kitchen?
  **B** Did they ................................................................ ?

**3 A** Someone brings her shopping to the house.
  **B** She ........................................................ to the house.

**4 A** A famous chef is making their wedding cake.
  **B** They ............................................ by a famous chef.

**5 A** Someone takes a photo of their family once a year.
  **B** They ..................................................... once a year.

**6 A** Does someone prepare her meals?
  **B** Does she ................................................................ ?

## Commands and instructions

**2** Complete the instructions with the correct form of the verbs in the box.

> accept   buy   not forget   not invite
> make   send   think

**How to plan the best party**

**1** First, ............................. about the number of people.

**2** ............................. too many.

**3** If friends offer to help, ............................. their offers.

**4** ............................. the invitations a couple of weeks before the date.

**5** ............................. the fresh food on the day of the party.

**6** ............................. simple dishes that don't take long to prepare.

**7** Finally, ............................. the neighbours may not like loud music!

## Listening Part 1

> • If there are two speakers, the information you need may come from either of them.
>
> • When you have chosen your answer, try to decide why the other two options are wrong.

 **Exam advice**

**1** For each question, choose the correct answer.

**1** What was the man unhappy with at the restaurant?

    **A**             **B**             **C**

**2** Where is the girl going?

    **A**             **B**             **C**

**3** What did the man forget?

    **A**             **B**             **C**

**4** What does the man want to borrow?

    **A**             **B**             **C**

**5** How much will the woman pay for the meal?

£17.70 A    £22.70 B    £45.40 C

**6** Where does the man want to go first this afternoon?

A    B    C

**7** Which film does the reviewer recommend?

A    B    C

## Writing Part 2 (An article)

**Exam advice**

- Imagine who will be reading your article. What do you think they find interesting?
- Try to use varied vocabulary and not to repeat the same words.

**1** Read this exam task.

You see this notice in an International English-language magazine.

**Articles wanted!**

**A HEALTHY LIFESTYLE**
What kind of things can you do to feel healthier?
Eat well, sleep well, do exercise – or all of these things?
Is it important to you to be healthy? Why? / Why not?
**The best articles will be published next month.**

Write your **article**.

Now match the questions (1–5) to the student's notes below.

**1** What can you do to feel healthier in general?
**2** Should you eat well?
**3** Should you sleep well?
**4** Should you do exercise?
**5** Why is it important to have a healthy lifestyle?

a FRESH FOOD

b ENJOY LIFE

c COMBINATION OF ALL THREE THINGS – DIET, SLEEP, EXERCISE

d SPORT – TWICE A WEEK

e 8 OR 9 HOURS

f EAT LOTS OF FRUIT AND VEGETABLES

g WALK NOT CAR

h FEEL HAPPY

i DON'T MISS IMPORTANT MEALS

**2** Read the student's article. Did he answer all the questions?

In my opinion, a healthy lifestyle is a combination of food, sleep and exercise. If you eat well but you don't do any exercise, you can't be healthy.

It's essential to eat fresh food. For example, I always buy meat from the butcher's, and I don't eat too much fast food. I also have fruit and vegetables with every meal. I think breakfast is an important meal if you want to have energy for the day.

You should also try to do exercise. Maybe do a sport twice a week or walk instead of going by car. If you are healthy, you will feel happy and enjoy life.

**3** Write your own answer to the task in Exercise 1 in about 100 words. Make notes, organise your answer in paragraphs and answer all the questions.

Looks amazing!

# 11 The natural world

**Exam advice**

- You won't hear the exact same words in the recording that you hear in the question and options.
- You have time before the listening starts to read the questions and options. Use this time to think about the words you might hear.

1 **For each question, choose the correct answer.**

You will hear an interview with a young man from Bermuda called Magnus, who helps to protect the oceans and the wildlife in them.

1 Magnus first became interested in the problem of pollution in the sea when
  A he found some examples of it.
  B he was given a book about it.
  C he attended a talk about it.

2 The first thing Magnus did after becoming a member of an environmental group was
  A to count the number of different plants.
  B to help scientists to get information.
  C to test new equipment.

3 Magnus learnt that people
  A don't realise the danger of some products.
  B don't know enough about how food becomes contaminated.
  C don't care about what they throw away.

4 What advice does Magnus give to people who want to help to protect sea life?
  A start an environmental organisation
  B avoid items with certain ingredients
  C stop eating fish

5 What does Magnus think has been his greatest achievement so far?
  A showing visitors to his island what the problem is
  B improving the beaches on Bermuda
  C encouraging more people to visit Bermuda's aquarium

6 What does Magnus want to do next?
  A work for an environmental charity
  B get a qualification
  C take part in environmental projects on his island

## Grammar
### The passive

1 **Rewrite the sentences to make them passive.**

1 Someone stole my wallet from my bag.
  My wallet ......................................... from my bag.
2 People don't use public phones any more.
  Public phones .................................... any more.
3 A loud noise woke them up.
  They ........................................ by a loud noise.
4 Lions often hunt zebras.
  Zebras ......................................... by lions.
5 Lots of people watched the wildlife documentary.
  The wildlife documentary ............................. by lots of people.
6 They created the national park in 1995.
  The national park ......................................... in 1995.
7 The wind didn't blow the tree down.
  The tree ......................................... by the wind.
8 They protect the animals from hunters.
  The animals ........................................ from hunters.

**2** Put the words in order to make questions.

1 the / was / When / aquarium / built / ?

..........................................................

2 organisation / was / set / When / up / the / environmental / ?

..........................................................

3 taken / for / the / Where / recycling / rubbish / is / ?

..........................................................

4 given / results / the / the / were / to / When / students / ?

..........................................................

5 are / used / the / What / machines / for / ?

..........................................................

6 animals / captured / are / How /the / ?

..........................................................

7 you / countryside / in / brought / Were / up / the / ?

..........................................................

8 animals / Are / the / well / looked / zoo / the / after / in / ?

..........................................................

**3** Complete the letter to a newspaper with the correct form of the verbs in brackets. Use the present or past simple passive.

# Letters

Dear Editor,

I am a resident of Hollyhill village, and I am writing to you to express my concern about the government's decision not to make the Black Mountain area into a National Park.

The park **(1)** ........................... (use) by many people for picnics at weekends and in summer. But if this area **(2)** ........................... (not / protect), then the animals will disappear. Last year many trees **(3)** ........................... (cut down) to make a road, and a fence **(4)** ........................... (built) along the road so animals can't cross it.

A project **(5)** ........................... (set up) by our local environmental committee to help protect the wildlife in our mountains, and last year many kilos of rubbish **(6)** ........................... (pick up) by volunteers, but if people **(7)** ........................... (not / prevent) from entering the area, then the problem will continue.

If this letter **(8)** ........................... (read) by lots of people who feel the same as us, maybe we can work together to solve the problem.

Yours sincerely,

John Tulley

**4** **Exam candidates often make mistakes with the passive. Underline and correct one mistake in each sentence.**

1 When was taken that photograph?
2 The houses were paint white.
3 I was enjoyed the trip to the island.
4 Children are not been allowed to see this film.
5 The book was writen 100 years ago.
6 The garden surrounded by a high wall.

## Comparative and superlative adverbs

**5** Complete the sentences with an adverb from the box in the comparative or superlative form.

badly   carefully   easily   fast
hard   quietly   slowly   well

1 The ostrich runs ........................... of all birds, but it can't fly!
2 I let my friend ask for the train tickets when we were in London because she speaks English ........................... than me.
3 You have to move ........................... through the jungle or you will frighten the animals away with the noise.
4 Next time, you should check your work ........................... . You made some basic mistakes.
5 The tiny rabbit ran ........................... than the others and was the last to get to the hole.
6 Jasmin found the way to the meeting point ........................... than she expected, so she arrived early.
7 The student who studied ........................... was given a grant for the next year.
8 Our team played ........................... in the group, so we didn't get into the semi-finals.

## Vocabulary
### Animals

**1** Find the words for eight animals. Then complete the sentences below.

| B | E | A | D | C | I | N | G | K |
|---|---|---|---|---|---|---|---|---|
| R | P | E | N | G | U | I | N | A |
| T | K | C | H | E | O | D | I | N |
| I | F | A | N | O | S | R | U | G |
| G | U | M | B | Y | T | C | M | A |
| E | P | E | E | L | R | A | T | R |
| R | F | L | A | M | I | N | G | O |
| L | G | A | R | T | C | I | S | O |
| B | E | L | E | P | H | A | N | T |

**1** An ............................ has a trunk and big ears.

**2** A ............................ can go a long time without drinking water.

**3** A ............................ is pink and often stands on one leg.

**4** A ............................ is a member of the cat family.

**5** An ............................ has a long neck and wings.

**6** A ............................ lays eggs and can swim.

**7** A ............................ likes eating honey.

**8** A ............................ stands on two legs and jumps.

### Noun suffixes

**2** Complete the sentences with a noun made from the word in brackets.

**1** Have you received ............................ of your flight from the airline yet? (confirm)

**2** We had a ............................ about the problem of global warming. (discuss)

**3** They sent us an ............................ to the conference. (invite)

**4** ............................ is a serious problem in many major cities. (pollute)

**5** The screen I ordered online was broken, so I asked for a ............................ . (replace)

**6** This app will give you the ............................ of a word in 50 different languages. (translate)

**7** The ............................ of the audience grew when they heard that the first prize was an African safari. (excite)

**8** The ............................ of technology has helped us to protect animals in danger of extinction. (develop)

**9** Good evening, I'd like to make a ............................ for four people for dinner on Friday, please. (reserve)

**10** Space ............................ started in the 1960s, when the first astronaut travelled outside the Earth's atmosphere. (explore)

**3** Correct the mistakes with nouns in these sentences.

**1** The scientists made an announceation that they had found a new species. ............................

**2** All children have the right to a good educateion. ............................

**3** After the completement of the project, he wrote a report. ............................

**4** One of the most important invents in history was the wheel. ............................

**5** Amy's disappointing was clear when she missed the trip to London. ............................

**6** The only entertaination in the town is the local cinema. ............................

## Reading Part 5

- Write the words you think are correct in the gaps on the question paper and read the text again to see if it makes sense.

- Carefully copy the correct letter onto the answer sheet afterwards.

**Exam advice**

**1** For each question, choose the correct answer.

### Rhinos

Rhinos are some of the largest animals in the world. They live in Africa and Asia in tropical rain **(1)** ............................ and grasslands. The biggest **(2)** ............................ can weigh 2,400 kilos, which is the weight of 30 men. Although they are very big and strong, they don't **(3)** ............................ other animals, but instead they feed on lots of grass and other plants. In fact, they spend all day and night eating. What rhinos really love is being in or near water, where they can **(4)** ............................ cool. They generally live on their own, except for the **(5)** ............................ relationship they have with oxpeckers. These are small birds that sit on rhinos and help keep them free of insects. Rhinos only have one **(6)** ............................ – humans, who kill them to take their horn. Since the beginning of the 20th century their population has fallen from 500,000 to only 29,000 now living in the wild.

| | A | | B | | C | | D | |
|---|---|---|---|---|---|---|---|---|
| **1** | A | trees | B | woods | C | coasts | D | forests |
| **2** | A | species | B | wildlife | C | range | D | set |
| **3** | A | chase | B | catch | C | hunt | D | benefit |
| **4** | A | keep | B | take | C | have | D | make |
| **5** | A | separate | B | unusual | C | complete | D | real |
| **6** | A | danger | B | competitor | C | enemy | D | injury |

# Writing Part 1

**Exam advice**

- Think about the tenses you need to use to answer the questions in the email. Is the information in the past, present or future? Try to use a variety of verb forms.

- Connect your ideas with words like *so*, *since*, *as*, etc.

**1** Look at the exam task and answer the questions.

1 What did you tell Freddie in your last email?

2 Which four things must you put in your reply?

Read this email from your friend Freddie and the notes you have made.

Write your **email** to Freddie, using **all the notes**.

---

**To:**

**From:** Freddie

Hi,

I'm happy to hear you've managed to get a few days off. If you haven't got other plans, would you like to stay at my place next weekend? — *Yes!*

While you're here, the environmental club I belong to needs some volunteers. We could either help pick up litter along the river or plant trees in a park for a few hours. Which activity would you prefer? — *Say which* We have to wear old clothes and boots for these kinds of activities. I have an extra pair of boots if you want to borrow them. — *No, because ...*

What else do you want to do during your stay? — *Tell Freddie*

All the best,

Freddie

---

**2** Read Martin's answer and choose the correct option in *italics*.

Hi Freddie,

**(1)** *I love / I'd love* to get together next weekend, especially as I **(2)** *haven't had / don't have* the chance to get out of the city for ages.

The environmental club sounds fun! I'd rather help to plant trees, I think. I **(3)** *did / have done* that last year in the park near my house and the trees **(4)** *already grew / have already grown* taller. I **(5)** *love / loved* nature, so I like to protect the environment.

Can we visit the national park near your village, too? I remember it was so beautiful last spring. We could take a picnic if the weather **(6)** *is / will be* nice.

Anyway, **(7)** *I'll be / I am* at your house early on Saturday morning.

I can't wait to see you!

Cheers,

Martin

**3** Read the answer again. Did Martin include all four points in the reply?

**4** Write your own answer to the task in Exercise 1 in about 100 words. Before you begin, look again at the exam instructions, then plan and write your email.

# 12 Express yourself!

**Exam advice**

- If you miss one of the words, just move on to the next question. You will hear the recording a second time.
- Check your answers carefully in the second listening.

**1** For each question, write the correct answer in the gap. Write one or two words or a number or a date or a time.

You will hear a woman called Jemma talking about a video-making course she went on last year.

## Jemma's video-making course

Jemma's visit to a (1) ........................... started her interest in film-making.

She attended the course on Saturday mornings except in the month of (2) ..........................., when she also went in the afternoon.

Examples of the videos they made are: giving advice about (3) ..........................., dance classes or performances of plays.

The groups had to take their own (4) ........................... to use in the videos.

She especially enjoyed the (5) ........................... at the end of the course.

She'd like to learn more about (6) ............................

---

## Vocabulary

### Collocations: using your phone

**1** Complete the sentences with a verb.

1 I always use my phone to ........................... the time. I don't have a watch.
2 I don't often ........................... friends. I prefer to send them a text message.
3 I like to ........................... games on my phone. I especially like *Clash Royale*.
4 I love to ........................... selfies when I go on a trip. I want to see myself with a memorable background.
5 I don't often ........................... online when I don't have wifi. It uses too much data.
6 I use Instagram to ........................... videos with my friends. We watch them and pass them on if they are funny.
7 I usually ........................... friends when I want to see them. I rarely phone them because a quick message is much easier.
8 I often ........................... music on my phone when I'm travelling on public transport – with headphones, of course!

### *ask*, *ask for*, *speak*, *talk*, *say* and *tell*

**2** Choose the correct option in *italics*.

1 Would you ever *say / tell / speak* a lie if it could help someone?
2 Sarah can *talk / tell / speak* Italian perfectly because she lived in Italy for 10 years.
3 Mark was tired when he got home, so he *asked / said / told* goodnight to everyone and went straight to bed.
4 Now I have social media, I don't *talk / ask / say* to my friends very often on the phone.
5 I was lost, so I went into a shop to *ask for / ask the / ask* help.
6 I wanted to *tell / say / talk* I was sorry, but Jordan didn't listen to me.
7 Can you *speak / ask / tell* me your surname?
8 My boss wants to *talk / say / ask* to me about my plans for next year.

## Negative prefixes

**3** Complete the sentences with the adjectives in the box and a negative prefix – *im-*, *in-* or *un-*.

> believable   comfortable   complete   correct
> expensive   friendly   patient   polite
> possible

1 It's ............................ to take the last biscuit on the plate.

2 We lost one of the pieces, so the puzzle is ............................ .

3 You have to wait. Don't be so ............................ !

4 It was an ............................ concert with amazing sound and a great audience!

5 If your answer is ............................ , then the other team gets a turn.

6 This problem is ............................ to solve. We'll never work it out.

7 The bed in the hotel was really ............................ , so I didn't sleep well.

8 Dancing is a fun and ............................ way to keep fit.

9 No one spoke to me at the party. They were really ............................ .

## Reading Part 4

- Look at linking words and expressions like *before that, afterwards, later, in addition* to help you decide which sentence is missing.

- Look at pronouns (e.g. *they / their / them; we / our / us*) in the sentences before and after the spaces to see if they make logical and grammatical sense.

**Exam advice**

**1** Five sentences have been removed from the text below. For each question, choose the correct answer. There are three extra sentences which you do not need to use.

A For this reason they are trained to find drugs or search for people.

B That's why they make good pets.

C These senses are used by different creatures for different purposes.

D Having this ability protects their young.

E This shows the others exactly where to go.

F For example, humans show how they feel about another person by kissing or shaking hands.

G Clearly, some of them have used it in the past.

H This included identifying colours, shapes and sizes as well as showing feelings.

# ANIMAL communication

Pet owners know very well that animals can communicate with humans and with each other, but scientists still find it difficult to explain how this happens.

Animals communicate through sounds, smells, movements and touch. **(1)** ............ For example, to tell a member of their species about food, or warn them of danger, or even just to play.

No one has ever proved that animals can really talk, although a famous parrot called Alex was trained to recognise and show knowledge about different objects. **(2)** ............ He also learnt and could say many English words, such as 'I love you', which he said to his trainer every night. Other birds cannot make human sounds, but they clearly use different noises or songs when they are in danger or want to attract a partner.

We also know that animals produce different smells or chemicals in order to communicate information to each other. They will use these to mark their territory or to say where there is food. Dogs are well-known for having a good sense of smell. **(3)** ............ They also get to know other dogs by smelling them first before they become friends!

Scientists have known for some time that when a bee has found a rich source of food, it goes back to its hive and performs a kind of dance. **(4)** ............ They don't need the bee that found the food to actually take them there.

Finally, a lot of animals use different parts of their body to communicate. **(5)** ............ Elephants will do something similar as they link their trunks to show friendship.

## Grammar
### Reported speech

**1** Rewrite the sentences in reported speech.

**1** The examiner said to us, 'You can't leave the room before the end of the test.'
The examiner said ..........................................................
.......................................................the room
before the end of the test.

**2** Jeff said, 'I don't want to go out late.'
Jeff said ..........................................................
.......................................................to
go out late.

**3** Martha said, 'We are leaving in the morning.'
Martha said ..........................................................
.......................................................in the
morning.

**4** He said, 'Zoe will come over at ten o'clock.'
He said ..........................................................
..........................................................
over at ten o'clock.

**5** She said, 'Harry's lived in that house all his life.'
She said ..........................................................
.......................................................in
that house all his life.

**6** Sue said, 'I enjoyed the trip very much.'
Sue said ..........................................................
.......................................................the
trip very much.

### Reported questions

**2** Correct the mistakes in the direct questions.

**1** John asked me if I was going to China.
John asked me, 'Were you going to China?'
..........................................................

**2** Gwen asked her boss when he would give her a day off.
Gwen asked her boss, 'When would you give me a day off?'
..........................................................

**3** Kevin asked Linda how many people Mia had invited to the party.
Kevin asked Linda, 'How many people have you invited to the party?'
..........................................................

**4** Anne asked Jack if he wanted to go to the beach.
Anne asked Jack, 'Do you wanted to go to the beach?'
..........................................................

**5** Robin asked me why I couldn't stay longer.
Robin asked me, 'Why can't I stay longer?'
..........................................................

**6** Jo asked Jenny where she had bought that dress.
Jo asked Jenny, 'Where do you buy that dress?'
..........................................................

### Reported commands

**3** Look at the instructions for taking an exam and complete the reported commands.

**1** 'Write clearly.'
The teacher told us ........................................
............................................... .

**2** 'Don't use a pen.'
The teacher told us ........................................
............................................... .

**3** 'Be careful with spelling.'
The teacher told us ........................................
............................................... .

**4** 'Don't worry about understanding every word.'
The teacher told us ........................................
............................................... .

**5** 'Guess the meaning.'
The teacher told us ........................................
............................................... .

**6** 'Don't forget to bring an identification document.'
The teacher told us ........................................
............................................... .

**4** Exam candidates often make mistakes with reported speech.
Underline the mistakes in the sentences and correct them.

**1** My teacher said me that my work was very good.
**2** I asked the shop assistant if she can help me.
**3** He told to me he would like to come and visit my country.
**4** They told me if I wanted to come to their house for dinner.
**5** She promised don't tell anybody.
**6** I called my friend and told him I found his camera.

## Indirect questions

**5** Complete the indirect questions.

1 What time is it?
Could you tell me ............................................................?

2 Can I take a photo?
I was wondering if ............................................................ .

3 Where is the IT department?
I'd like to know ............................................................ .

4 How often do you look at your phone?
Could I ask you ............................................................?

5 Where does Thomas live?
Do you know ............................................................?

## Writing Part 2 (A story)

- The story should have a beginning, middle and end. Use paragraphs to make this clear.

- You can write what people say as well as what they do in the story. You can use direct or reported speech.

**Exam advice**

**1** Look at this exam task and a student's answer. Put the paragraphs in the correct order.

Your English teacher has asked you to write a story. Your story must begin with this sentence.

*I was excited when I read the text message!*

Write your **story** in about **100** words.

**A** ☐

I shouted to my husband, 'Tom! I'm going to Paris to play in the championship!' but he didn't answer. I ran downstairs to find him. Unfortunately, I didn't see that my dog was coming out of the living room.

**B** ☐

I fell hard on the floor and heard a horrible noise. Then, my arm started to hurt. Tom came out of the kitchen, looked at it and said, 'I think you've broken it!' That was the end of my trip to Paris.

**C** ☐

I was excited when I read the text message! It was unbelievable! The volleyball club had chosen me to play in the team for the European championship.

**2** Write the sentences with the correct punctuation.

Example:
Katie asked where are you going
*Katie asked, 'Where are you going?'*

1 Lucas said I've hurt my leg
............................................................

2 The police officer asked when did you arrive home
............................................................

3 Marina announced I'm going to America
............................................................

4 Charlie replied I don't know
............................................................

**3** Write the sentences in Exercise 2 in reported speech.

Example:

1 ............................................................
............................................................

2 ............................................................
............................................................

3 ............................................................
............................................................

4 ............................................................
............................................................

**4** Now answer this exam task. Write three or four paragraphs: the beginning, the middle and the end.

Your English teacher has asked you to write a story. Your story must begin with this sentence.

*I slowly opened the box and looked inside.*

Write about 100 words. Try to use direct or reported speech in your story.

## My life and home

**1** Complete the crossword.

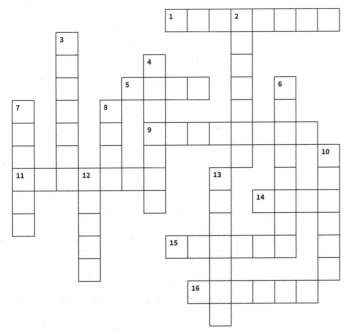

**Across**

**1** My mum always sits in her favourite ............... when she wants to watch TV. (8)

**5** We went through the front door into the ............... . (4)

**9** Danny, can you put the lemonade glasses in the ............... in the living room, please? (8)

**11** On weekdays, we eat in the ..............., not in the dining room. (7)

**14** The three friends sat together on the ............... to play the video game. (4)

**15** There is space in our ............... for two cars. (6)

**16** The ............... is in the bathroom. We don't have a separate one. (6)

**Down**

**2** The chair in my room is a bit hard, so I use a ............... when I sit on it. (7)

**3** It's cold, so I'll put an extra ............... on your bed. (7)

**4** Our hotel room had a lovely ..............., where we could sit outside and see the sea. (7)

**6** I have too many clothes to fit in that small ............... . (8)

**7** Don't put your hand on the ............... . It's still hot. (6)

**8** I filled the ............... with warm water and got in. (4)

**10** He almost fell when he ran down the ............... . (6)

**12** My grandmother has a lovely old ............... of drawers where she keeps everything. (5)

**13** My favourite place in my house is my ............... because I have all my things there. (7)

**2** Exam candidates often make spelling mistakes.
<u>Underline</u> the mistakes in the sentences and correct them.

**1** In my bedroom I have a bed, a desk, a cupbord and a wardrobe.

**2** The furnature in my grandma's house is made by hand.

**3** In the hall, we've got a large mirrow on the wall.

**4** We don't have a dinning room in our new flat.

**5** Under the window there's a wooden chest of draws.

**6** There's a small kichin in my house, which I share with three other people.

**3** Choose the correct option in *italics*.

**1** I've got an important meeting *on / in* Thursday morning.

**2** Shall we meet *on / at* the station this afternoon?

**3** We heard the news on the radio *at / in* breakfast time.

**4** There were no more chairs, so I had to sit *on / in* the floor.

**5** I waited *on / at* the bus stop, but the bus didn't come.

**6** We went swimming *in / at* the sea.

# 2 Vocabulary extra

## Making choices

**1** Complete the crossword.

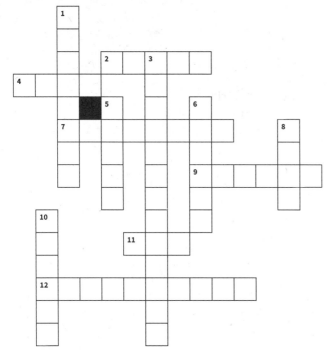

**Across**

**2** The people who work at the college are very nice – both the teachers and the administration ............... . (5)

**4** I hate my job, so I'm going to .............. it next month and look for something different. (4)

**7** At the end of the year, he got a prize for being the best .............. in the company. (8)

**9** Many people in the UK .............. when they are 65 and enjoy a relaxed life. (6)

**11** Before university, I want to take a .............. year and travel the world. (3)

**12** My course is great because we have classes, but we also get work .............. in a company in our second year. (10)

**Down**

**1** Would you like to have your own .............. or work for someone else? (8)

**3** I'm going to study abroad, so I need to look for .............. where I can stay for the year. (13)

**5** I'm going to .............. for a job with a multi-national company. I hope I get it! (5)

**6** Ellie's studying for a history .............. at Durham University. (6)

**8** Please complete the application .............. and send it together with your CV. (4)

**10** His .............. as a footballer ended when he hurt his back. (6)

**2** Write the past simple form of these verbs.

**1** fail ...........................
**2** learn ...........................
**3** pass ...........................
**4** take ...........................
**5** miss ...........................
**6** set off ...........................
**7** study ...........................
**8** teach ...........................

**3** Complete the sentences with the correct form of the verbs from Exercise 2 in the past simple.

**1** Last month, all the students on my course .............. an important exam. Most of us .............., so we don't have to study in the summer holidays.

**2** Yesterday, I .............. for work at 7 o'clock. But the bus was late, so I .............. the beginning of an important meeting.

**3** Although I .............. all night for the exam last week, I .............. because I was too tired to concentrate.

**4** In my first year at business school, the teachers .............. us economics. I also .............. to write reports.

**4** Correct the underlined mistakes in the sentences.

**1** I'd like a job where I do a lot of money. ..............

**2** We all make fun when we go out at the weekends. ..............

**3** I like to pass the afternoon with my family. ..............

**4** My teacher learned me a lot of useful things last year. ..............

**5** My brother made his driving test yesterday, but I don't know if he passed. ..............

**6** You were late this morning. Did you lose the bus? ..............

**5** Match the sentences 1–9 with the functions A–C.

**A** Making a suggestion
**B** Agreeing
**C** Disagreeing

**1** How about having a break now?
**2** I don't agree with you.
**3** Great idea. I totally agree.
**4** Shall we talk about something different now?
**5** Good point. We can do that.
**6** I'm not sure that's a good idea.
**7** Let's choose the second option.
**8** Why don't we decide later?
**9** You're quite right. So do I.

## Having fun

**1** Complete the sentences with the words in the box.

> bake board brush cameras chain digital fire
> helmet performance practise queen recipe
> sleeping bag water watercolours wetsuit

**1** I fell off my bike when the ............................................. broke, but luckily I was wearing a ............................................. .

**2** I sometimes ............................................. a cake without following a ............................................. as an experiment. It usually tastes good!

**3** I like to use a thin ............................................. when I paint with ............................................. .

**4** Although it was cold, we were comfortable by the ............................................. , but I was happy I had a good ............................................. once we got in the tent.

**5** Of course I only take ............................................. photos. The old-fashioned ............................................. are too expensive and more complicated to use.

**6** I have to ............................................. every day for hours before I give a public ............................................. .

**7** I moved my ............................................. to the square in the corner of the ............................................. and then I realised that was not a good move.

**8** I love the feeling of silence under the ............................................. , and I have a special ............................................. to keep me warm.

**2** Now match the sentences in Exercise 1 to the activities A–H.

**A** camping ..............
**B** diving ..............
**C** playing the piano ..............
**D** photography ..............
**E** playing chess ..............
**F** cooking ..............
**G** cycling ..............
**H** painting ..............

**3** Complete the dialogues with a verb from the box. Sometimes more than one answer is possible.

> afford enjoy fancy feel like finish go off
> look forward to promise put down
> remember run out of suggest take

**1** **A:** I've got a headache, so I don't ............................................. going to the cinema tonight.

  **B:** Never mind. I'll ............................................. going when you are better.

**2** **A:** What do you think I should do to relax?

  **B:** I ............................................. doing yoga. It certainly makes me feel calm.

**3** **A:** My old camera doesn't ............................................. very good photos.

  **B:** Can't you ............................................. to buy a new one? Why don't you look in the sale?

**4** **A:** You must ............................................. to buy some bread today.

  **B:** OK. I ............................................. to do it on my way home after work.

**5** **A:** When you go to the shops, can you get me a pen? Mine is going to ............................................. ink.

  **B:** OK! I'll do it after I ............................................. cleaning the car.

**6** **A:** I ............................................. going skiing again this winter.

  **B:** Really? I thought you would ............................................. skiing after your accident last year.

**7** **A:** I want to ............................................. my name for the university basketball team this year.

  **B:** Good idea! I'm sure you'll ............................................. playing for them.

# 4 Vocabulary extra

## On holiday

**1** Complete the email with the words or phrases in the box.

> dry   good time   hang   hire   journey   market
> original   peace and quiet   sightseeing
> snorkelling   souvenirs   trip

Hi Eva,

How's the summer going? I'm having a **(1)** ............................ here in Cancún, Mexico with Bill and Joe. The weather is warm but wet because it's the rainy season. We go out in T-shirts, but it rains every day, so it's difficult to stay **(2)** ............................ . It doesn't matter, it's not cold!

There are things for everyone to do here. On Monday we decided to **(3)** ............................ bikes and we cycled along the coast. Joe wanted to go **(4)** ............................ yesterday, so I went with him and we saw some amazing fish. Bill decided he wanted some **(5)** ............................ , so he stayed in the hotel, reading by the pool.

Tomorrow the hotel has organised a **(6)** ............................ to see some pyramids, so we're planning to go **(7)** ............................ there and also visit a town where we can look around a street **(8)** ............................ and go shopping. Maybe I'll buy some **(9)** ............................ . I'll get you something **(10)** ............................ , not just a T-shirt! The only bad thing is the **(11)** ............................ home – 16 hours in a plane is exhausting.

I hope you're having a good holiday too and get to **(12)** ............................ out and do some interesting and fun things.

Lots of love,

Fred

**2** Complete the crossword.

### Across

**3** Kings and queens sometimes live in this beautiful building. (6)

**5** Local people can go to the town ............... to talk to somebody official about their neighbourhood. (4)

**8** An example of this could be a statue of a king or an important building. (8)

**9** My sons go to a ............... club every Saturday to play table tennis or table football and meet friends. (5)

**10** I love ............... . I enjoy sleeping in a tent. (7)

### Down

**1** There's lots you can do in the ............... centre: swim, go to the gym and use the climbing wall. (6)

**2** I had to go up to the fourth floor of the ............... store to find shoes and bags. (10)

**4** In an art ............... you can see wonderful paintings and special exhibitions. (7)

**6** There are noisy machines in this place so all the ............... workers wear ear protection. (7)

**7** There's a beautiful one in the town square – they turn on the water three times a day. (8)

## Different feelings

**1** Match the emojis to the feelings.

> annoyed   cheerful   confused   embarrassed
> frightened   jealous   miserable   surprised

| 1 | 2 | 3 | 4 |
|---|---|---|---|
|  |  |  |  |
| ................... | ................... | ................... | ................... |

| 5 | 6 | 7 | 8 |
|---|---|---|---|
|  |  |  |  |
| ................... | ................... | ................... | ................... |

**2** Complete the table with adjectives from the box.

> afraid   angry   ashamed   bored   brave   cute
> depressed   disappointed   funny   generous
> grateful   guilty   pleased   satisfied

| Positive adjectives | Negative adjectives |
|---|---|
| | |
| | |
| | |
| | |
| | |
| | |

**3** Complete the sentences with an adjective from Exercise 2. If necessary, change the form of the adjective from *-ed* to *-ing*.

1 I think the news on TV is really ........................... . The reporters say nothing interesting.
2 My husband brought home a ........................... puppy last week. It looks like a little ball of fur.
3 I was really ........................... when my sister broke my phone. I shouted at her.
4 I ate the last biscuit, and then I felt ........................... because my little brother was hungry.
5 My uncle always invites the whole family to have lunch in a restaurant on his birthday. He's very ........................... .
6 Ellie was ........................... when the stranger gave her the money she had dropped in the street.
7 I think he's ........................... to swim in the sea in winter.
8 Scoring the winning goal in a match is very ........................... .

**4** Choose the correct option in *italics*.

1 I had a very *tired / tiring* day shopping today.
2 Eva was really *surprised / surprising* when she got the message.
3 I love horror movies or series that are *frightened / frightening*.
4 After work I like to listen to *relaxing / relaxed* music.
5 I was *amazed / amazing* when I managed to beat my brother at tennis.
6 His message was very *confused / confusing*, so I didn't know what to do.

**5** Complete the sentences with a preposition.

1 The whole class is crazy ........................... the new video game.
2 You shouldn't be afraid ........................... that bully.
3 I feel nervous ........................... speaking in public.
4 My sister was very pleased ........................... her new phone.
5 Jake was embarrassed ........................... his old clothes.
6 You must be very proud ........................... your son getting such a good job.

# 6 Vocabulary extra

**1** Complete the crossword.

**Across**

**1** I went to the comic ............... in Barcelona to see all the new Japanese magazines and characters. (4)

**7** After the first half of the concert there was an ............... , so we went to the café. (8)

**9** The cinema is sometimes called the big ............... . (6)

**11** Steven Spielberg is a well-known film ............... . (8)

**12** The circus is my favourite type of ............... . (13)

**Down**

**2** I want to be an actor because I love performing in front of an ............... . (8)

**3** ............... to the museum is £5 for adults and £2 for children. (9)

**4** Actors stand on the ............... to perform in a theatre. (5)

**5** After a performance, journalists sometimes write a ............... to give their opinions. (6)

**6** I love the TV ............... about a hospital and the people who work there. (6)

**8** The play is very popular, so you have to ............... tickets early. (4)

**10** We sat in the front ............... of the theatre so we could see the actors perfectly. (3)

**2** Complete the sentences with the correct word.

**1** I like classical music and singing, so I enjoy going to the *opera / musical*.

**2** Have you ever seen your favourite singer perform *live / alive*?

**3** The actor appeared on a *chat / reality* show yesterday to talk about her new film and her life.

**4** The *crowd / audience* at the football match went crazy when their team scored a goal.

**5** I helped to make the *scenery / tickets* for the drama club play by painting trees and flowers.

**6** My girlfriend really loves classical dancing, so we go to the *ballet / concert* once a year.

**3** Complete the sentences with words from the box.

> been   found out   gone   got to know
> known   met

**1** I've ............... how to get cheap tickets for the concert. A friend of mine works with the band.

**2** Jessie has ............... to Germany for the whole summer. She won't be back until September.

**3** Have you ever ............... a famous footballer in real life?

**4** We've ............... our neighbours for many years.

**5** I really like Katie now I've ............... her better. I thought she was a bit strange at first.

**6** Danny's ............... to America several times because he has an uncle there.

## Getting around

**1** Match the words from box A with the words from box B to make compound words. Then label the photos with the compound words.

1

2

3

4

5

6

**A**

| car | rail | round | thunder | traffic | under |

**B**

| about | ground | jam | park | storm | way |

**2** Complete the sentences with the singular or plural form of a compound word from Exercise 1.

**1** You shouldn't walk over the ............................................ because there are too many cars going round it.

**2** I prefer to travel by ................................................ in a big city because it's faster than the bus.

**3** Take the train and I'll meet you outside the ............................................ station.

**4** I don't mind ............................................ , but I'm afraid of lightning.

**5** You can always find a space in the big ............................................ at the supermarket.

**6** There was a huge ............................................ in the city centre because of the big football match. Nobody could move.

**3** Complete the holiday blog with the sentences below. Write A–E in the gaps.

### Can the weather spoil a holiday?
*Read our readers' comments*

| **Mick:** | You can't always expect the weather to be fine here in June. Most of the time **(1)** ............... . Still, we had umbrellas and it was good not to be sightseeing in the heat. |
| **Rebecca:** | I wanted to climb the mountain, but there was a huge storm. **(2)** ............... , but I was happy I watched from the safety of my room. |
| **Louis:** | Our plan was to go to the coast and walk along the beach to see the birds and watch people sailing, but that day **(3)** ............... , and we couldn't see more than two metres in front of us. |
| **Anna:** | The best part of the trip was when **(4)** ............... and we could go skating on the lake. It was very cold, but we wore warm clothes and had a lot of fun. |
| **Finley:** | Although the forecast said it was going to be cold and wet, in fact **(5)** ............... nearly the whole time we were here, so we went to the beach every day. |

**A** the temperature was below freezing

**B** the sky was cloudy and there were showers

**C** it was warm and dry

**D** the thunder and lightning were really impressive

**E** it was really foggy

# 8 Vocabulary extra

## Influencers

**1** Match the opposites.

| | | | |
|---|---|---|---|
| 1 | miserable | **a** | hard-working |
| 2 | modern | **b** | rude |
| 3 | lazy | **c** | smart |
| 4 | stupid | **d** | quiet |
| 5 | noisy | **e** | old-fashioned |
| 6 | polite | **f** | cheerful |

**2** Complete the sentences with words from Exercise 1.

1 They are always talking loudly. They are ............................. .

2 Carmen walked along the road smiling and singing to herself. She was ............................. .

3 I want a phone that uses the latest technology. I want a ............................. phone.

4 Elly never helps with cleaning our flat and just lies on the sofa all weekend. She is ............................. .

5 Her shoes look like the ones my mother wore when she was young. They are ............................. .

6 Hugo always says 'please' and 'thank you'. He is ............................. .

7 Henry looks really unhappy. He is ............................. .

8 They tried to push to the front of the queue. They were ............................. .

**3** Complete the word puzzle and find the word in grey.

1 She doesn't worry about giving presentations. She is .............. .

2 He always gives money to charity. He is .............. .

3 She never offers to help anyone. She is .............. .

4 She doesn't say much. She's very .............. .

5 He worries a lot about problems. He is .............. .

6 They always help their neighbours. They are .............. .

7 He doesn't like to talk in public. He is .............. .

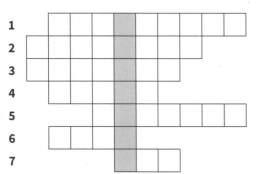

**4** Answer the questions about Danny, Jamie, Olivia and Sara.

1 Who has got a moustache? .............................

2 What is Olivia's h air like? ........................... , ...........................
and ...........................

3 Who has got a scar? .............................

4 Who has got broad shoulders? .............................

5 What is Danny's hair like? ........................... and ...........................

6 What is Sara's hair like? ........................... and ...........................

7 Who is slim? ........................... and ........................... .

8 Who is bald? ...........................

**5** Choose the correct option in *italics*.

1 Caitlin was late for work because she didn't hear her alarm, but she *made up* / *found out* an excuse that the bus didn't come so she had to walk.

2 I spent my childhood in the countryside, where I *brought up* / *grew up* on a farm.

3 My best friend and I didn't *take up* / *get on* very well with each other when we were younger, but now we are always together.

4 Harry wanted to have his own business, but he *ran out of* / *set up* money after a few months and had to close the company.

## Stay fit and healthy

**1** Complete the sentences with one or two words.

**1** He's .................................................. his finger.

**2** She's got a ............................................... .

**3** He's having an ............................. .

**4** He's taking some ............................. .

**5** He's got a .............................. on his arm.

**6** She's putting a .............................. on his wound.

**2** Complete the sentences with the correct option.

**1** I used to *go / play / have* swimming every day when I was younger.

**2** The athletes couldn't run because the *pitch / court / track* was too wet.

**3** We *hit / drew / scored* in the final 30 seconds and won the match.

**4** There is a badminton *court / pitch / match* at my local sports centre where we can practise.

**5** My brother *did / went / made* skiing last winter.

**6** The golfer *kicked / hit / threw* the ball 200m.

**7** Do you often *practise / do / go* sport?

**8** She likes to go to yoga classes in the *stadium / gym / court* once a week.

**9** We play soccer on an artificial *track / pitch / court* at school.

**10** If you try hard, I'm sure you'll *win / beat / draw* the other team.

**3** Match the words in the box with the pictures. Write down a sport that uses each type of equipment.

> bat   gloves   helmet   kit   net   racket
> swimsuit   trainers

**1** helmet — cycling, ice hockey, American football

**2** ........................................................................

**3** ........................................................................

**4** ........................................................................

**5** ........................................................................

**6** ........................................................................

**7** ........................................................................

**8** ........................................................................

# 10 Vocabulary extra

## Looks amazing!

**1** Complete the crossword.

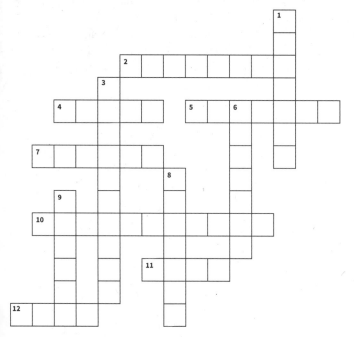

**Across**

2 the person who buys something in a shop (8)
4 A dentist looks after your ............... . (5)
5 You can study or read books here. (7)
7 You can buy cakes or bread here. (6)
10 This person will cut or dye your hair. (11)
11 a piece of paper that shows how much you have to pay (4)
12 the person who cooks the food in a restaurant (4)

**Down**

1 something you buy at a reduced price (7)
3 a person who doesn't eat meat (10)
6 a person who sells meat (7)
8 a person who sells medicine (7)
9 a place where you have your car repaired (6)

**2** Complete the sentences with the correct word.

1 I had my broken phone *mended / reserved*.
2 Can we *borrow / lend* your tent for the camping trip?
3 I *caught / complained* to the manager about the meal.
4 Chloe *did / made* an appointment at the hairdresser's.
5 You'll need to *book / hire* your holiday soon.

**3** Put the food words in the correct category. Some words belong to more than one category.

> apple  beef  bread  butter  cake  cheese  chicken
> chips  chocolate  cucumber  eggs  grapes
> lettuce  mushrooms  pasta  peanuts  pear
> rice  spinach  steak  sweets  tuna  yoghurt

| Proteins | Carbohydrates | Fruit & vegetables | Milk & dairy products | Fats & sugars |
|---|---|---|---|---|
|  |  |  |  |  |

**4** Match the words to the pictures.

> chopsticks   fork   frying pan   glass   jug   knife
> plate   spoon

.........................  .........................  .........................  .........................

.........................  .........................  .........................  .........................

# 11 Vocabulary extra

## The natural world

**1** Label the pictures with the words in the box.

> beach  cliff  hill  island  lake  rock  stream
> valley  waterfall  wood

**2** Complete the sentences with the correct word.

1 Many people in big cities have health problems because of the *prevention* / *pollution* caused by car fumes.
2 An alternative energy source could be *solar* / *sun* energy, which is clean.
3 If we build more houses in the countryside, the *live* / *wild* animals will lose their habitat.
4 Reusing objects for different purposes helps reduce *weight* / *waste*.
5 Governments create national parks to *protect* / *prevent* animals.
6 Tigers are in *danger* / *worry* of extinction.
7 You should give up having baths to *keep* / *save* water.
8 One of the *aims* / *finals* of the project is to create more green areas in the city.

**3** Complete the text with words from the box and the correct suffix: *-ation*, *-ion* or *-ment*.

> announce  create  discuss  educate  enjoy
> excite  invite  reduce

### 1 April

The **(1)** ............................................. that was made last week by the President has surprised many teachers and students. She reported that after a long **(2)** ............................................. the government has decided to replace all course books with tablets. The **(3)** ............................................. of new online material will be the responsibility of local authorities. This news has caused great **(4)** ............................................. among the students and it is certain that the **(5)** ............................................. ............................................. they will get from using the new technology will benefit their learning because they will also have fun. Some teachers have already received an **(6)** ............................................. to attend training courses and most of them are pleased with the change to the **(7)** ............................................. system. The **(8)** ............................................. in paper needed for books will also help the environment.

## Express yourself!

### 1 Complete the sentences with the correct word.

1 Megan often tells *lies / jokes / messages* about why she is late for class and the teacher never believes her.

2 We will send you *a letter / an email / a selfie* in the next 30 seconds to confirm your registration on the course.

3 You need to ask *to your manager / for your manager / your manager* if you can miss work tomorrow.

4 When I was younger, I couldn't *say / speak / talk* any French, but now I know a lot.

5 I'm not sure of the *vocabulary / communication / meaning* of the word 'geek'.

6 My brother went to the USA and learnt lots of *slang / chats / translations* from his friends, like the word 'sweet', which means 'nice' or 'good'.

7 I have to go. Please *say / tell / speak* goodbye to your assistant for me.

8 If you need anything, *say / speak / ask* the shop assistant for help.

### 2 Match the beginnings and endings of these sentences.

1 You'll need a password to
2 If you receive a strange email,
3 I haven't got enough memory on my phone to
4 There are several film blogs where you can
5 It's not a good idea to give any personal information when you
6 Choose the correct option and
7 It's an online form, so you don't need to
8 You can use an emoji to show your feelings when you

a drag it to the space provided.
b print anything.
c connect to the internet in this café.
d post your comments.
e send messages.
f delete it immediately.
g install that app.
h chat online.

### 3 Complete the sentences with the words from the box. Use a negative prefix where necessary.

> complete   expensive   fair   healthy   patient
> perfect   polite   successful

1 Eating too many sweet things is ............................ .

2 You have to be ............................ when waiting at the doctor's.

3 It was ............................ to give him extra work when he had done nothing wrong.

4 It's important to be ............................ when you talk to older people.

5 I've just started playing tennis, so I don't need an ............................ racket.

6 Daniel went for a job interview, but he was ............................ . He'll have to try harder next time.

7 You can't be right all the time. Nobody is ............................ .

8 The story was ............................ because it didn't have an ending.

# Workbook Answer key with audioscripts Units 1–12

## Unit 1
### Vocabulary

**1**

| | | | |
|---|---|---|---|
| **1** duvet | **2** pillow | **3** sink | **4** fridge |
| **5** microwave | **6** towel | **7** mirror | **8** tap |

**2**

**1** at  **2** in  **3** on  **4** in  **5** in  **6** at  **7** on  **8** on

**3**

**Countable:** beach, bus, cooker, day, floor, friend, game, hall, house, tap, time (for occasions, eg *four times*)
**Uncountable:** electricity, food, furniture, homework, make-up, money, rain, shampoo, space, time (period of time)

### Reading Part 5

**1** C  **2** A  **3** D  **4** B  **5** C  **6** B

### Listening Part 2

**1** B  **2** A  **3** C  **4** B  **5** C  **6** C

---

**Track 2**

**Narrator:** For each question, choose the correct answer.

**1**

**Narrator:** You will hear a mother and her son talking about his old school books.

**Boy:** Mum, where should I put my old school books? I've hardly got any space, so I need to get rid of some.

**Woman:** Well, they are sometimes useful when you want to check something, but Aunt Sylvia asked me if we could let your cousin Harry have them this year.

**Boy:** That's not a bad idea. I can always borrow one back if I ever need it.

**Woman:** All right, just put them in the cupboard in the hall for the moment and I'll tell Sylvia to pick them up.

**Boy:** OK, Mum.

**2**

**Narrator:** You will hear a boy telling his friend about helping at home.

**Girl:** Hi, Luke. Shall we go into town this morning?

**Boy:** I'd love to, but my mum wants me to help her move stuff. She's clearing out the garage, and she can't do it by herself. We're going to look through all the old boxes of photos and toys. I'm actually looking forward to seeing what's there. It would be quicker if Jack helped, but he has to study for a university exam at a friend's house.

**Girl:** Yeah, my brother's always got an excuse too!

**Boy:** I think it's true this time! We can meet tomorrow, OK?

**3**

**Narrator:** You will hear two college students talking about a trip.

**Woman:** Hey Pete, are you coming on the trip to the mountains tomorrow?

**Man:** Well, I signed up for it and I even bought some new walking boots. Actually, I think they're a bit small, so I'll have to change them. But that's not important, because in the end I can't go.

**Woman:** Why not?

**Man:** I promised to take my girlfriend to see her parents. I got the wrong day when I told her about the trip and now I can't change anything.

**Woman:** That's a pity. But you've got those boots for the next time!

**Man:** I have!

**4**

**Narrator:** You will hear two friends talking about a TV series.

**Man:** I saw that new series last night. It was amazing!

**Woman:** I know, it's really interesting, isn't it? The things that happen seem so true to life – in fact, they're a bit like my family sometimes!

**Man:** You're not serious! They have too many problems to be true, but I agree the brother and sister play their parts really well.

**Woman:** Yeah, I think they're convincing. I'm looking forward to the next episode. I want to know what happens in the end to their friend who disappeared.

**Man:** I reckon the sister knows where he is.

**Woman:** We'll see if you're right next week!

**5**

**Narrator:** You will hear a woman talking to a friend about a house.

**Man:** So, how's your new house?

**Woman:** Well, it's OK. The kids have got their own rooms and my husband has put a gym in the garage. You know, with an exercise bike and other machines.

**Man:** Wow! That's great!

**Woman:** Yeah, but I prefer going out to the gym. It also means we have to leave the car outside. I don't really like leaving it on the street, especially because we live on a busy main road. I have to park it round the corner. But at least I can walk to the office.

**Man:** That's better than when you had to take the train every day!

**6**

**Narrator:** You will hear two friends talking about a shopping centre.

**Woman:** Have you been to the new shopping centre yet?

**Man:** Yes, I went yesterday. It's got loads of great shops, hasn't it?

**Woman:** Well, if you like clothes, but there isn't much else there. I think our area needs more places to eat and I expected a cinema or something for entertainment.

**Man:** You're right, but anyway, it's easy to get to on the bus and there's a car park.

**Woman:** True. It only took me ten minutes last Saturday, but I won't be going much. I prefer the local shops on the High Street.

## Grammar

**1**
1 They occasionally eat in a restaurant.
2 I go skiing once a year.
3 He hardly ever takes photos on holiday.
4 I eat a good breakfast every day.
5 She doesn't often go on holiday abroad. / She doesn't often go abroad on holiday.
6 Some people read the newspaper almost every day.
7 I take my dog to the park most days.
8 They are never at home in the mornings.

**2**
1 b   2 c   3 c   4 c   5 b   6 a   7 a   8 a

**3**
| | | |
|---|---|---|
| 1 is snowing | 2 know | 3 opens |
| 4 hates | 5 misses | 6 wear |
| 7 are growing | 8 is learning | 9 is getting |
| 10 watch | | |

**4**
| | | |
|---|---|---|
| 1 am ('m) spending | 2 feel | 3 have |
| 4 go | 5 start | 6 finish |
| 7 attend | 8 am ('m) not studying | 9 am ('m) sitting |
| 10 don't have | 11 are ('re) doing | 12 means |
| 13 am ('m) taking | 14 are you doing | 15 Do you want |

## Writing Part 1

**1**
1 d   2 c   3 a   4 b

**2**
**Inviting:** Would you like to come to my party? Do you want to go to the theatre tonight?
**Suggesting:** Shall we go to the exhibition? Why don't we have a barbecue?
**Asking for information:** Which is the best place to visit? What kind of films do you like?

**3** (*Sample answer*)

Dear Robin,

Thanks for your email and your invitation. Jack is very kind! I'd love to go on holiday with you to the coast.

I think the second week is better for me, if you don't mind. My father's birthday is on the 5th August and I want to be at home for that.

I don't often go to the beach, so I'd like to sunbathe and swim in the sea. We could also try some of the local food. You know I love going to restaurants.

Shall we get him some plates for the kitchen? My local shop sells some really nice ones.

I'm looking forward to seeing you.

Love,

## Unit 2
## Vocabulary

**1**
| | | |
|---|---|---|
| 1 take, pass | 2 fail | 3 work, study, teach, learn |
| 4 lose | 5 set off, miss | |

**2**
1 ~~wins~~ → earns   2 ~~do~~ → make   3 ~~earn~~ → spend   4 ~~made~~ → did
5 ~~do~~ → spend   6 ~~spent~~ → took   7 ~~makes~~ → takes   8 ~~earned~~ → won

## Reading Part 6

1 of   2 for   3 have / 've   4 the   5 but   6 me

## Grammar

**1**
1 spent, took, Did (you) go, didn't have
2 got / did, Did (she) earn / make, had
3 went, Did (you) make, met
4 didn't do, made, didn't spend, had

**2**
| | | |
|---|---|---|
| 1 used to enjoy | 2 was giving, stopped | 3 Did you spend |
| 4 was raining, came | 5 was talking, received | 6 didn't use to let |
| 7 was concentrating, didn't realise | 8 decided, were shopping | |

**3**
| | | |
|---|---|---|
| 1 set off | 2 was shining | 3 looked / was looking |
| 4 arrived | 5 was running | 6 felt |
| 7 stopped | 8 noticed | 9 were coming |
| 10 didn't walk | 11 began | 12 was still raining |
| 13 didn't matter | 14 had | 15 felt / were feeling |

## Listening Part 1

1 B   2 A   3 C   4 B   5 A   6 B   7 C

---

**Track 3**
**Narrator:** For each question, choose the correct answer.

**1**
**Narrator:** What job does the student want to do after university?
**Man:** It's really hard to decide what to do after university. As a kid I wanted to be a pilot. I thought engineering was good for that, but you need to train a lot after university, so now I'm not so keen. I like design but most jobs involve sitting in front of a computer all day, and I don't want to do that the rest of my life. I'm interested in helping others to learn, so I think I'll try to stay on where I am.

**2**
**Narrator:** Where are the woman's glasses?
**Woman:** Have you seen my glasses? I think I left them on the kitchen table last night, but they're not there now.
**Man:** You usually leave them in the bathroom when you're doing your make-up. Where did you have them yesterday?
**Woman:** I was on the computer after lunch, but in the evening I decided to read on the sofa downstairs for a while.
**Man:** Look, they're just where you were sitting yesterday evening!

**3**
**Narrator:** When do the students have to give their final presentation?
**Girl:** Hi Danny. I'm just phoning you because I was ill yesterday, and I missed the meeting about our final presentation. Did the teacher say when the presentation is?
**Boy:** Yes, she wanted us to do it next Tuesday but a lot of us have an exam that day, so she changed it to the end of the week.

| | |
|---|---|
| **Girl:** | Oh, that's great. If it's on Friday, we'll have more time to prepare. |
| **Boy:** | Don't forget we've got to do our project work for Thursday morning as well. |
| **Girl:** | Oh no! |

**4**

| | |
|---|---|
| **Narrator:** | Which activity does the man recommend? |
| **Woman:** | What activity do you think I should do at the sports centre this year? |
| **Man:** | Well, last year I played badminton. It was a friendly group, but a lot of the adults stopped going, so there may be too many children. |
| **Woman:** | Hmm, that's not so good. I'd like to meet people as well as get some exercise. |
| **Man:** | In that case, kick-boxing is popular, especially with women. |
| **Woman:** | That sounds difficult. |
| **Man:** | Not really, and it helps reduce stress! You'll meet more people there than if you only do something like swimming on your own. |

**5**

| | |
|---|---|
| **Narrator:** | What did they do when it started to rain? |
| **Man:** | How was your trip to the mountains, Jenny? |
| **Woman:** | It was great at first. It was really hot, and we found a fantastic place to have lunch under some trees. But in the afternoon the weather changed, and it began to rain really hard. It was a long way to the car, but we found a cave where we waited for it to stop. The sun came out again on the way back, so we didn't get wet at all. |

**6**

| | |
|---|---|
| **Narrator:** | What was the first prize in the competition? |
| **Woman:** | Now, we have good news. The winner of our nature photography competition this year is Mark Young from Bristol University photography club. His photo of sunlight on the trees in the park means that the club will get a video camera. The second prize is cinema tickets for four people. This went to Jenny Jackson from Bath University for her photo of a snail. Thanks to all the university clubs that took part. They will all receive a certificate. |

**7**

| | |
|---|---|
| **Narrator:** | Why did the man go to bed late? |
| **Woman:** | You look tired, Sam. Did you go to bed late last night? |
| **Man:** | Yeah, I was watching that TV series about detectives in New York when my brother phoned. |
| **Woman:** | The one who lives in Australia? |
| **Man:** | That's right. He didn't remember that it was late for us, but anyway we were talking until after midnight. |
| **Woman:** | Is he OK? |
| **Man:** | He's having a great time although he's working hard in a restaurant every evening. |

## Writing Part 2 (An article)

**1**

What makes a good university or college, teachers, facilities, something else and the social activities a university or college should offer.

**2**

Tick 1, 3, 4, 5, 7 and 8

**3**

*Students' own answers*

**4**

**1** opinion     **2** sure     **3** think / agree     **4** agree

**5** *Sample answer*

A good university

There are several reasons why a university or college is a good place to study. I think that the lectures are very important, but there are other things that make the experience special. For example, if you are studying science, it's good to have laboratories and equipment to do practical work.

However, in my opinion I think that one of the most important experiences at university is meeting other people, so the social activities it has are vital. Some people like sport, others like dancing. There should be activities for all kinds of people so that they can have fun after studying and make friends. (108)

## Unit 3
## Reading Part 3

**1** C   **2** D   **3** B   **4** A   **5** B

## Vocabulary

**1**

| | | | |
|---|---|---|---|
| **1** in front of | **2** above | **3** on / to | **4** behind |
| **5** under | **6** between | **7** inside | **8** in |

**2**

| | | | |
|---|---|---|---|
| **1** ran out of | **2** sign up | **3** hang on | **4** join in |
| **5** give up | **6** set off | **7** go on | **8** look after |

**3**

| | | |
|---|---|---|
| **1** rides – cyclist | **2** plays – (chess) player | |
| **3** takes – photographer | **4** goes – diver | **5** plays - musician |

## Listening Part 4

**1** A   **2** B   **3** C   **4** B   **5** C   **6** A

| **Track 4** | |
|---|---|
| **Narrator:** | For each question, choose the correct answer. You will hear a radio interview with a young magician called Megan. |
| **Interviewer:** | Today we're going to talk to a young woman with a very exciting hobby. During the day she works in an office, but in her spare time she's a very talented magician. Tell me, Megan. How did you become interested in magic? |
| **Megan:** | Well, my interest in magic began when I was only five years old and I got a magic game as a present. Then after seeing a magician at a birthday party when I was eight I knew that this was what I wanted to do. My friends used to call me Magic Megs and I became a member of a magician's club to learn more. |
| **Interviewer:** | What did you learn in the club? |
| **Megan:** | Of course, I learnt lots of new tricks. I also realised that not many girls did magic because everyone else there was a boy! I was amazed! I used to practise for hours every day, and I entered the Young Magician of the Year competition when I was 16. No girl had ever won this competition at the time, so I was really proud when I came second. |
| **Interviewer:** | So, do you work as a magician now? |

| Megan: | Not often, it's not easy to earn enough money working as a magician, and I do have other interests apart from performing. I studied animal conservation at university, and during the day I work in an office helping with environmental projects. I can't do many shows because it takes me ages to prepare and practise for each one. |
|---|---|
| Interviewer: | What do you think has been your greatest achievement? |
| Megan: | I love my work helping animals and I got good qualifications from university, but I was so pleased and amazed when I was chosen to be the secretary of The Magic Circle, one of the most important magicians' clubs in the world. I was the first woman to be elected in an organisation that has traditionally been run by men. |
| Interviewer: | What style of magic do you do? |
| Megan: | Well, I like to combine magic with another of my hobbies, dancing. I've loved this since I was a child as well. Some magicians talk a lot when they're doing magic, but I prefer to perform with music and I like wearing fantastic costumes and make-up. |
| Interviewer: | So, are you happy with your life now? |
| Megan: | Well, … I'll worry about the future when it comes. I won't ever give up magic, but I love my job too. There's something magical about nature, perhaps more than any trick I could do. In both cases I feel I'm doing something good, making people happy when they see me perform and helping protect the world we live in when I'm at work. |

## Grammar

**1**
**1** being    **2** to meet    **3** to go    **4** to drive    **5** doing
**6** reading    **7** seeing    **8** speaking    **9** to come

**2**
**1** a    **2** b    **3** b    **4** a

**3**
**1** meeting    **2** taking    **3** to eat    **4** to ask
**5** to bring    **6** to put    **7** going    **8** dancing

## Writing Part 2 (A story)

**1**
*Students' own answers*

**2**
Example A is better. It answers the questions in Exercise 1. In example B, the second sentence does not follow on logically from the given sentence because it doesn't talk about anything amazing but rather it describes a normal situation.

**3–5** *Sample answer*

I walked into the room and everyone stopped talking. All my family were there in the living room and they looked at me in surprise. I didn't know why.

I sat down and said, 'What's the matter?' My mother said, 'James, what happened to your hair?' I went out to the hall and looked in the mirror. My hair was green! Then, I remembered washing my hair with a new shampoo the night before.

I went back into the room and saw my little sister laughing. She showed me a little green bottle and ran out of the living room. I ran after her, really angry.

# Unit 4
# Grammar

**1**
**1** freezing    **2** totally    **3** absolutely
**4** extremely    **5** bad

**2**
**1** best    **2** quick    **3** easiest
**4** earlier    **5** more important    **6** worst

**3**
**1** ~~more~~    **2** ~~that~~ → than    **3** ~~larger~~ → largest
**4** ~~longer~~ → long    **5** ~~thing~~ → things

**4**
**1** a lot / far / much smaller
**2** as far … as
**3** much / far / a lot more expensive than
**4** as big as
**5** a bit / a little / slightly longer … than
**6** much / far / a lot later than
**7** much / far / a lot nearer … than
**8** a bit / a little / slightly cheaper than
**9** as small as

## Reading Part 1

**1** C    **2** A    **3** B    **4** A    **5** C

## Vocabulary

**1**
**1** b    **2** c    **3** f    **4** d    **5** h    **6** a    **7** g    **8** e

**2** (*suggested answers*)

| wildlife holiday | camping trip | city break | beach holiday |
|---|---|---|---|
| enjoy nature see animals | make a fire sleep in a tent | buy souvenirs go sightseeing | go snorkelling sunbathe |

**3**
**1** journey    **2** trip    **3** travel    **4** travel
**5** journey    **6** trips

## Listening Part 3

**1** 1 / one / an hour    **2** music    **3** tents
**4** (fantastic) robots    **5** Monday(s)    **6** T-shirts

---

**Track 5**

**Narrator:** For each question, write the correct answer in the gap. Write one or two words or a number or a date or a time. You will hear a guide talking about tours of a film studio.

**Guide:** This week we have three different tours for you to try. They are all based on films made in these studios.

First, the *Robert the Bruce* tour, especially popular with fans of history. There's an hour-long tour in the morning at ten. You'll visit the palace built for the film and you can use headphones to hear actors' voices from different moments in the story. Afterwards, there's a 15-minute documentary about the different places where the film is set, with fantastic scenes of mountains in Scotland and life in the old city of York, accompanied by music from the film.

Another exciting tour is to the Native American camp that was built for *The Totem Men* – the film about the history of Native Americans in the northwest USA. This tour takes 30 minutes and you go into tents where you watch actors cooking, making clothes and preparing to hunt, showing you how families lived at that time.

Finally, our most popular tour is the 45-minute visit to the science-fiction world of *Ricky Ranger*. You will love this tour because you can see inside Ricky's spaceship and meet some of the team that made the film. They'll explain how the fantastic robots in the film were created using the latest Japanese technology.

If you want to complete your day with a meal, visit our Oakwood cafeteria. We serve healthy salads and burgers every day except Mondays. On Wednesdays there's a special offer of two pizzas for one. Don't forget to visit our gift shop to pick up a free poster. We also sell a wide range of T-shirts for children and adults. Finally, you can collect the photos of your visit from the office by the entrance.

We look forward to welcoming you to the studio soon.

## Writing Part 1

**1**
Tick 1, 2, 4, 6 and 7

**2**
**1** pretty    **2** amazing    **3** excellent / amazing
**4** delicious    **5** clean / warm    **6** long
**7** historic / pretty / amazing / fascinating

**3**
**1** ~~absolutely~~ → extremely    **2** ~~fasinating~~ → fascinating
**3** ~~amazed~~ → amazing    **4** ~~historical~~ → historic
**5** ~~beatiful~~ → beautiful    **6** ~~a bit~~

**4** *Sample answer*

Dear Toni,

It's fantastic you are going to visit my country as it's an amazing place and there are a lot of exciting things to do. The only problem is that it's enormous, so you can't see it all!

I think the best place to go is the south coast. It has a lot of historic villages, with lovely white houses, and there are monuments from ancient times, which you can visit.

It also has some wonderful beaches where you can go swimming and diving, and you can go on a boat trip to the beautiful islands together.

I hope you enjoy it!

Love,

## Unit 5
## Vocabulary

**1**
**1** disappointed    **2** jealous    **3** mean
**4** afraid    **5** embarrassed    **6** fond
**7** nervous    **8** ashamed

**2**
**1** angry with    **2** afraid of    **3** bored with/of
**4** ashamed of    **5** pleased with    **6** depressed about
**7** sure of/about    **8** crazy about

**3**
**1** generous    **2** miserable    **3** funny
**4** complicated    **5** fantastic    **6** positive
**7** relaxed    **8** ordinary

**4**
**1 a** boring **b** bored    **2 a** embarrassing **b** embarrassed
**3 a** relaxing **b** relaxed    **4 a** excited **b** exciting
**5 a** amusing **b** amused

## Reading Part 4

**1**
Yes, the writer enjoyed the experience.

**2**
**1** G    **2** D    **3** H    **4** A    **5** B

## Grammar

**1**
**1** could, can't    **2** can, might    **3** can't, might
**4** may, might    **5** Can, can

**2**
**1** shouldn't    **2** mustn't    **3** have to
**4** ought to    **5** don't have to    **6** must

## Listening Part 2

**1** C    **2** B    **3** A    **4** C    **5** B    **6** C

**Track 6**

**Narrator:** For each question, choose the correct answer.

**1**

**Narrator:** You will hear two friends talking about a basketball match.

**Woman:** Hi, Jake, did you go to the match yesterday?

**Man:** Yeah, but it was a bit disappointing.

**Woman:** Why, what happened?

**Man:** Well, it was quite exciting to begin with, but then Sam Turner fell and hurt his leg. He's going to be off playing for a month – just when we need him for the final next week. You know he's our star player.

**Woman:** Did your team win?

**Man:** Only by one point. They usually play much better than that.

**2**

**Narrator:** You will hear a woman talking to a friend about moving home.

**Man:** Hi Amelia. I haven't seen you for ages! Are you enjoying sharing a flat at university?

**Woman:** Well, it's not bad. The flat is nice and although the bedrooms are fairly small, mine's fine.

**Man:** Have you seen your friends much, now you're living in a different place?

**Woman:** You know, before I moved I thought that might be a problem, but we're right next to the station and there's a direct train back to my home town as well as buses to the city centre, so I needn't have worried. We all met up last weekend, which was fun.

**3**

| | |
|---|---|
| **Narrator:** | You will hear a student talking to a friend about a website. |
| **Man:** | Hey Jasmin, you know that project on pollution in cities we have to do next week? |
| **Woman:** | Yeah. I'm worried about where to get information. It's not easy to find what we need. |
| **Man:** | Well, I think I've found the perfect place. It's a site for students, and it's got pictures we're allowed to download for university work. |
| **Woman:** | Great! So we can use those for the presentation. What about the text we have to write? |
| **Man:** | The website can help with that too because there are sections about nearly all the cities in our project. |
| **Woman:** | So we only have to find a bit of information somewhere else. |
| **Man:** | That's right. |

**4**

| | |
|---|---|
| **Narrator:** | You will hear two friends talking about a party. |
| **Man:** | The party at Leo's house was fun, wasn't it? |
| **Woman:** | Yeah, I had a great time, good food, good music and you know I love dancing. |
| **Man:** | I know! You didn't stop most of the evening. It was tiring just watching you! |
| **Woman:** | Well, I did talk to people too. Did you chat to Lucy. She told me all about her trip to India last year. It was fascinating. |
| **Man:** | No, but I met a boy from Germany who is here for a month staying with Kevin. |
| **Woman:** | Oh, I could have practised speaking German with him. |
| **Man:** | You were too busy dancing! |

**5**

| | |
|---|---|
| **Narrator:** | You will hear a student telling a friend about a board game. |
| **Girl:** | My cousins came over yesterday and brought that new board game. You know, the one everyone is crazy about. |
| **Boy:** | Oh yeah, it's great. I played it at Ryan's house all afternoon last Sunday. |
| **Girl:** | That's the problem. It takes *hours* to play it, so you can't do anything else, and people take ages to decide their next move while everyone else just waits. Still, they're all trying to distract each other by chatting about different things, which is quite funny. My cousins have been playing it for the last month, so they're real experts, but I had to really concentrate. |

**6**

| | |
|---|---|
| **Narrator:** | You will hear two friends talking about a sports centre. |
| **Man:** | I went to the new sports centre last week. Have you been? |
| **Woman:** | Yes, I think it's amazing. There's lots to do and it's not too expensive. |
| **Man:** | The classes aren't that cheap. I wanted to do Pilates, but I don't think I can afford it. |
| **Woman:** | Still, there's lots on offer and the booking system is so efficient it's easy to sign up for whatever you want. |
| **Man:** | That's true. I also met some of the trainers, who were very friendly. |
| **Woman:** | But the receptionist is a bit rude, don't you think? She didn't smile once and ignored me when I asked for information. |

## Writing Part 2 (A story)

**1**

**Place(s):** at work / on holiday / at home / in a sports match
**People:** my husband / a teacher / a shop assistant / my family / a police officer / a friend / my wife
**Problem(s):** I lost something / I forgot something / I missed the bus/train / I broke something
**Feelings:** angry / miserable / sad / nervous / depressed / embarrassed / disappointed

**2**
**1** E   **2** A   **3** D   **4** B   **5** C

**3** *Suggested answers*
**1** nervous          **2** angry          **3** embarrassed

**4** *Sample answer*

I remember the day I met my hero. It was a beautiful day. My best friend and I wanted to climb the mountain behind my house, so we left early in the morning with sandwiches and water in our rucksacks.

At about 12 o'clock we were feeling hungry and tired, so we stopped to have a rest. Suddenly, we heard a voice singing. The sound was coming from the trees behind us. It was a wonderful sound. We stood up and went to see who it was.

What a surprise! It was my favourite singer. He was walking in the mountains, too. I was so excited because he's always been my hero.

## Unit 6
## Vocabulary

**1**
**1** quiz show          **2** the news          **3** comedy series
**4** cooking show       **5** reality show      **6** wildlife documentary
**7** sports programme

**2**
**1** perform            **2** book              **3** screen
**4** subtitles          **5** admission         **6** stage
**7** Refreshments       **8** interval          **9** live
**10** tickets

**3**
**1** known; met         **2** got to know him   **3** gone
**4** been               **5** been              **6** found out

## Reading Part 2

**1** D   **2** H   **3** E   **4** C   **5** B

## Grammar

**1**
**1** for          **2** already       **3** just       **4** since   **5** yet
**6** already      **7** just          **8** yet

**2**
**1** have you known      **2** took          **3** haven't been
**4** learnt/learned      **5** have ('ve) told    **6** went

**3**
**1** ~~have had~~ → had   **2** ~~He's bought the tickets yet~~ → He's already bought the tickets / He hasn't bought the tickets yet.
**3** ~~gone~~ → been   **4** ~~are~~ → have been   **5** ~~know~~ → have / 've known
**6** They **have** / **'ve** already seen the film.

# Listening Part 1

1A  2C  3B  4A  5C  6B  7A

**Track 7**

**Narrator:** For each question, choose the correct answer.

**1**

**Narrator:** Which programme did the man enjoy?

**Man:** I saw a great programme on TV yesterday.

**Woman:** Was it that new comedy?

**Man:** Well, I started watching that, but it wasn't very funny, so I switched channels and saw something else. It was a competition between four people to see who could make the best cake, but at the same time they had to explain what they were doing.

**Woman:** So you learnt something useful as well?

**Man:** Yes, the winner could answer all the questions about how to do it well. It was good, so I might make one myself.

**2**

**Narrator:** How much did the ticket cost?

**Woman:** Did you get a ticket for the concert?

**Man:** Yes, I got it online. It was quite expensive. I didn't want to pay £30, but there were no cheaper tickets.

**Woman:** I thought they cost £20. That's what the advert said.

**Man:** That was the one I wanted to get, but there weren't any left. Actually, that was all the money I had, so my sister lent me some money. Now I have to give her £10 back when I get paid next week.

**Woman:** Never mind. It'll be worth it!

**3**

**Narrator:** Where does the woman want to watch the football match?

**Man:** Are you going to watch the match on Saturday? I've got tickets for the game.

**Woman:** I'm not keen on watching it live because you can't see so well and it's cold at the moment. Anyway, I've already told Ollie that I'm going to watch it at his house. He's got a big-screen TV, so we can see it really well there. Last time, I tried watching the final on my computer, but my internet connection isn't good, so I missed the second half.

**Man:** How annoying!

**4**

**Narrator:** Which shirt does the man buy?

**Shop assistant:** Can I help you?

**Man:** Yes, I'm looking for a present for my brother. I think he'd like a shirt.

**Shop assistant:** What about this one? We've got it in all sizes.

**Man:** Well … he doesn't like stripes, and I think it's too formal. Have you got anything with short sleeves?

**Shop assistant:** There's this one that has two colours or this other plain one.

**Man:** Have you got the plain one in a small size?

**Shop assistant:** Oh, I'm sorry, we haven't. We may get some more soon.

**Man:** It's for tomorrow, so I'll take the other short-sleeved one then.

**5**

**Narrator:** Who is the man's tennis coach?

**Man:** Look over there, Sal. There's my new tennis coach.

**Woman:** Where? Is he the one with glasses and a black jacket?

**Man:** No, he's much older than that. Remember I told you he's been teaching at another club for years. He's the one with the beard and glasses.

**Woman:** Oh yes, he's talking on his phone.

**Man:** Yeah. He does that in our lessons as well! I'm not too happy about it.

**Woman:** Oh, that's a pity. It's hard to find good coaches, isn't it?

**Man:** Yeah!

**6**

**Narrator:** What has the girl forgotten?

**Woman:** Hi Mum, it's Laura. I'm on the coach with the rest of the team, but I've got a bit of a problem. The thing is I think I've left my swimming costume at home. I remember seeing it on the bed with my towel, but I don't remember putting it in my sports bag. I looked in my bag to check I'd got my ticket, and that was when I realised. Is there any chance you could bring it to the pool for me? *Please.* Can you call me as soon as possible?

**7**

**Narrator:** When did the concert finish?

**Man:** How was the concert yesterday?

**Woman:** It was good, but we didn't get home until really late, about midnight, I think.

**Man:** Oh, I thought it started quite early.

**Woman:** Yes, but they had a problem with the sound system at the concert, so it didn't end until 11, and then I had to wait half an hour for the bus. Luckily, I was with Hannah, so I didn't have to wait on my own.

**Man:** That's good, but you must be tired today.

**Woman:** Yes, I am!

# Writing Part 2 (An article)

**1**

**1** Have you ever seen a live basketball match?

**2** Why do people like going to the cinema at the weekend?

**3** Do you prefer going out or staying at home on a Saturday night? / Do you prefer staying at home or going out on a Saturday night?

**2**

**A** 3   **B** 2   **C** 1

**3**

**1** TV and film (cinema)   **2** He talks about watching a comedy show with his wife, and about why he enjoys going to the cinema.

**3** a question at the beginning of the article

**4** *Sample answer*

Do you like Saturday nights? I do, because there is always something fun to do.

A great way to spend the evening is going to watch sport. In my town there is always a football or basketball match at the sports centre. The atmosphere is exciting and I can meet my friends there.

If you want to watch a film, I think it is better to go to the cinema. You can go with family or friends, it doesn't matter. Don't you like eating popcorn and watching a romantic film? The big screen is amazing and much better than sitting at home alone.

Going out on Saturday night is fantastic!

# Unit 7
## Reading Part 1

1 C  2 A  3 B  4 A  5 C

## Vocabulary

**1**
| | | | |
|---|---|---|---|
| 1 frost | 2 showers | 3 foggy | 4 ice |
| 5 freezing | 6 thunderstorms | 7 rainy | 8 sunshine |
| 9 windy | 10 snowy | | |

**2**
| | | |
|---|---|---|
| 1 sunny | 2 temperature | 3 thunderstorm |
| 4 freezing | 5 weather | 6 raining |
| 7 foggy | 8 lightning | |

**3**
1 signpost; crossroads    2 sightseeing; guidebook; suitcases
3 overnight; campsite; backpack

## Listening Part 4

1 A  2 B  3 A  4 C  5 A  6 C

> **Track 8**
>
> **Narrator:** For each question, choose the correct answer. You will hear an interview with a student called Adam, who is going on a trip to the desert this summer.
>
> **Interviewer:** Good morning. Today we're going to talk to Adam Gill, who has come to tell us about his plans for this summer. Adam, I've heard that you're going to the desert.
>
> **Adam:** Yes, I'm going to spend two weeks in the Sahara Desert in Morocco with a group from university. We're all medical students, and we'd like to learn how the people there manage their health in difficult conditions. There are plans to build a new medical centre there because the current building is rather old and not big enough for all the patients.
>
> **Interviewer:** And what's your job going to be?
>
> **Adam:** Well, I'm the official photographer! My plan is to take photos and make a video there. We want to show people back home what's happening and try to raise money for the medical centre. I'll start from when we get off the plane, although the longest part of the journey will be overnight in a lorry, so I don't suppose I'll be able to do much then.
>
> **Interviewer:** And will you need a lot of equipment?
>
> **Adam:** Not really. A friend has lent me a video camera – it works better than my phone – and I've got a great digital camera that my parents gave me. I'll have to be careful though, because it might be hard to charge the batteries. I think the power is only on for a few hours in the evening.
>
> **Interviewer:** Will you need anything else? If it's hot, you won't need heavy clothes.
>
> **Adam:** Well, it does get quite cold at night, so I'll have to take a warm jacket, but I won't take many clothes. It's more the heat of the day that worries me because we have to wear long-sleeved shirts to protect ourselves from the sun.
>
> **Interviewer:** What about food?
>
> **Adam:** I've heard that Moroccan food is delicious, but the desert area is very dry and not much grows there. Most of our food will come with us in the lorry, so we don't use what little food the local people have there.
>
> **Interviewer:** So, are you excited about the trip?
>
> **Adam:** Of course! But I'm a bit nervous as well. I'm really not sure what it'll be like. It'll be my first time abroad, in fact, but a friend who went last year has told me the people are really friendly, even though he couldn't speak their language. He said if you don't mind not having a comfortable bed, then it's an amazing experience.

## Grammar

**1**
| | | |
|---|---|---|
| 1 too hot | 2 old enough | 3 too far |
| 4 clever enough | 5 too dark | 6 warm enough |
| 7 too small | 8 too many | |

**2**
| | | | |
|---|---|---|---|
| 1 fairly | 2 really | 3 quite | 4 really |

**3**
| | | | | | |
|---|---|---|---|---|---|
| 1 into | 2 out of | 3 by | 4 on | 5 on | 6 off |

**4**
| | | | |
|---|---|---|---|
| 1 I'll bring | 2 starts | 3 I'm playing | 4 is going to get |
| 5 does your train arrive | 6 I'll see | | |

**5**
| | | |
|---|---|---|
| 1 am ('m) going to see | 2 will ('ll) get | 3 am ('m) going to visit |
| 4 will ('ll) help | 5 will ('ll) call | 6 will ('ll) have |

## Writing Part 1

**1**
| | | | |
|---|---|---|---|
| 1 to | 2 sunny | 3 for | 4 sunglasses |
| 5 will ('ll) be / would be / could be | | 6 saw | |
| 7 in | 8 will ('ll) buy | | |

**2** *Sample answer*

Hi Alex,

It was great to hear from you. Thanks for reminding me about Lucy's birthday! I like your ideas, but it's better to go to your house because I think the restaurant will be too expensive for some people. I'm going to the cinema on Sunday afternoon, but I'm free on Saturday. Is that a good day for you?

I'm not sure what we can give Lucy. I know she likes music. Maybe we can buy her an Ed Sheeran CD because he's her favourite singer. I can go to the music shop tomorrow. Do you want to come with me?

Lots of love,

# Unit 8
## Vocabulary

**1**
| | | | |
|---|---|---|---|
| 1 make up | 2 brought up | 3 grew up | 4 ran out of |
| 5 got on | 6 found out | 7 took up | 8 set up |

**2**

| | | | |
|---|---|---|---|
| **1** strict | **2** lazy | **3** clever | **4** quiet |
| **5** generous | **6** rude | **7** anxious | **8** confident |

**3**

| | | | |
|---|---|---|---|
| **1** cheerful | **2** unreliable | **3** helpless | **4** beautiful |
| **5** unpleasant | **6** dishonest | **7** successful | **8** helpful |
| **9** impatient | **10** unfriendly | | |

**4**

| | | |
|---|---|---|
| **1** long, straight, dark | **2** short, curly, broad | **3** blonde, pale |
| **4** wavy, grey, beard | **5** bald, moustache | |

## Reading Part 6

| | | | | | |
|---|---|---|---|---|---|
| **1** how | **2** If | **3** has | **4** them | **5** than | **6** at |

## Grammar

**1**

| | | |
|---|---|---|
| **1** gets (1) | **2** would ('d) tell (2) | **3** go (1) |
| **4** Would you travel (2) | **5** will give (1) | **6** wakes up (0) |
| **7** wouldn't do (2) | **8** find (0) | |

**2**

| | | | |
|---|---|---|---|
| **1** If | **2** unless | **3** if | **4** when |
| **5** unless | **6** when | **7** when | **8** unless |

**3**

| | | | |
|---|---|---|---|
| **1** g – if | **2** f – unless | **3** d – unless | **4** c – if / when |
| **5** b – when | **6** e – if / when | **7** a – unless | **8** h – unless |

**4**

**1** came → come   **2** Did → Would   **3** Unless → If / has – hasn't
**4** doesn't → didn't / she'd → she'll   **5** will → would / won → wins
**6** When → If

## Listening Part 3

| | | |
|---|---|---|
| **1** Wales | **2** shape | **3** chemicals |
| **4** (five-litre) boxes | **5** 25,000 | **6** supermarkets |

**Track 9**

**Narrator:** For each question, write the correct answer in the gap. Write one or two words or a number or a date or a time. You will hear a lecturer talking to a group of students about a young couple who have set up a fruit juice business.

**Lecturer:** Maciek and Karina are two young entrepreneurs who are running a fruit juice business. Although they are originally from Poland and Lithuania, they studied for their degrees in Wales. Then they decided to stay there and start their own company because the business opportunities were better than back home.

The idea for their business began when they realised that a lot of fruit was being wasted because it's too small, too big or it isn't the right shape for sale in shops. This fruit tastes fine and gives the juice its natural colour, but farmers can't sell it directly to supermarkets and greengrocers. This means they often have to throw away a lot of their produce.

So the young couple decided to use this fruit to make juice. This has helped the farmers and provides a healthy fruit drink made from apples or strawberries. The company only uses natural ingredients and the juices are free of chemicals.

Maciek and Karina are also concerned about other environmental issues, such as the containers the juice comes in, so the juices are delivered in glass bottles that can be recycled. When they set up the business, in 2016, they sold juice in five-litre boxes, but then they changed to glass to reduce plastic waste.

They started the business by asking for help online and they received £2,500 in gifts from people who liked their idea. Later, they won £5,000 prize money for a business competition. After this, they were successful in getting a loan of £25,000 from a government organisation so the business could really begin to grow.

At the moment most of their customers are restaurants and catering companies, but they hope to expand to supermarkets in the future. They also support food charities because the aim of the company is to make not only money but also a better world.

## Writing Part 2 (An article)

**1**

**Spelling: 1** ofen → often   **2** funn → fun   **3** Fisics → Physics
**4** habilities → abilities   **5** freind → friend
**Punctuation: 1** dont → don't   **2** england → England
**3** holiday's → holidays   **4** *habilities → habilities,*   **5** Hes – He's

**2** *Sample answer*

I am lucky because I have lots of friends. A good friend is kind and helpful when you have problems. A good friend can be smarter than you or not as clever as you, but he or she always has time to listen. Sometimes, I just need someone to talk to.

I think you can relax with a good friend. You can just be together and have fun. It doesn't matter where or when. My friends don't all have the same hobbies. I like people that are different from me, who can give me new ideas or show me a new activity.

## Unit 9
## Listening Part 2

| | | | | | |
|---|---|---|---|---|---|
| **1** A | **2** B | **3** A | **4** B | **5** C | **6** A |

**Track 10**

**Narrator:** For each question, choose the correct answer.

**1**

**Narrator:** You will hear a man talking to a friend about their exercise class.

**Woman:** Hi Josh. What happened to you last Monday? You didn't come to the yoga class.

**Man:** Yeah, I'd had flu the weekend before, but because I was feeling better that day I thought I'd go. Then I got a message from my son to say his car had broken down, so I had to go and pick him up. It took me longer than I expected, and it was too late to go by the time I got home.

**Woman:** Oh no! Are you coming tonight? I can give you a lift if you want.

**Man:** That would be great, thanks.

**2**

| | |
|---|---|
| **Narrator:** | You will hear two friends talking about a table tennis competition. |
| **Man:** | You know there's a table tennis competition next Saturday. Do you want to be my partner? |
| **Woman:** | I'm not sure. You're much better than me. |
| **Man:** | Oh, come on. Anyway, it's not about winning. We'll all play a few games and there's food and drink. Everyone from the club will be there. |
| **Woman:** | I haven't seen some of them for ages, so that'll be fun. |
| **Man:** | Yeah, I usually spend Saturday mornings cleaning the house, so it'll be good for me to do something different too. |

**3**

| | |
|---|---|
| **Narrator:** | You will hear a woman telling her friend about a football match she went to. |
| **Man:** | Hi Lizzie, how was the match on Saturday? |
| **Woman:** | Well, it was OK, but I was a bit disappointed. |
| **Man:** | Why? What happened? Did your team lose? |
| **Woman:** | Yes, but that wasn't the problem. It was raining the whole match too, but luckily we had seats under cover so we kept dry. The thing is my brother had invited one of his friends to come with us and he spent the whole match shouting in my ear. I couldn't concentrate on the game and nearly missed the goal our team scored. |
| **Man:** | What do you expect at a football match? Maybe you should watch it on television next time! |

**4**

| | |
|---|---|
| **Narrator:** | You will hear two friends talking about a trip to an art gallery. |
| **Man:** | So what did you think of the art gallery? |
| **Woman:** | Well, I had a good time in the end. But I thought the summer exhibition of modern art would be better. I've seen a few of the pictures in other shows. |
| **Man:** | Oh, I missed it last year, so I thought the art was pretty unusual. That guide gave us some useful information, she told us more than just the name of the artist and the date. But I didn't think the pictures were organised very well. |
| **Woman:** | True. It wasn't always easy to see with those lights, but she did make it more entertaining. |

**5**

| | |
|---|---|
| **Narrator:** | You will hear a boy talking to his mother. |
| **Man:** | Hi, Mum. I'm home! |
| **Woman:** | Where have you been? I was getting worried. |
| **Man:** | I'm really sorry. I had a problem with my phone. I put it in my coat pocket and left it in the locker in the changing room when we went to play badminton. Harry's brother gave me a lift to the station and we were halfway there when I remembered my coat. By then it was too late to go back because the sports centre had closed. Plus the train was late and no one would let me use their phone to call you. |

**6**

| | |
|---|---|
| **Narrator:** | You will hear two friends talking about going skiing. |
| **Man:** | Hi Alicia, guess what! I'm going skiing this weekend! What do I need to take? |
| **Woman:** | Well, warm clothes, especially gloves and a hat. I don't think you need to get any expensive equipment until you know if you like it or not. You can rent skis quite cheaply. |
| **Man:** | I'm scared I might break a leg, or crash into someone and hurt them. |
| **Woman:** | Don't worry. If you don't mind falling sometimes – beginners always do – and just relax, you won't hurt yourself. As for other people, if they can ski better than you, then they have to move out of your way. |

## Vocabulary

**1**
**1** beat, football    **2** drew, athletics    **3** bat, baseball
**4** gloves, skiing    **5** racket, tennis    **6** score, volleyball

**2**
**1** bike    **2** rollerblading    **3** skateboard
**4** surfers    **5** exercise    **6** Mountain biking
**7** breath    **8** exhausted

**3**
**1** b   **2** d   **3** c   **4** g   **5** h   **6** a   **7** e   **8** f

## Reading Part 3

**1** C   **2** D   **3** C   **4** B   **5** D

## Grammar

**1**
**1** who/that    **2** whose    **3** when    **4** who
**5** where    **6** which

**2**
**1** who/that lives in the flat next door.
**2** whose mother was my nurse in hospital.
**3** when our team won the cup.
**4** where my parents got married.
**5** who is a pilot

**3**
**1** which → who / that    **2** students who / that use
**3** there    **4** her    **5** who's → whose

**4**
**1** had('d) had    **2** had('d) finished / finished
**3** did you go    **4** had seen    **5** got    **6** had('d) hurt

## Writing Part 2 (A story)

**1**
**1** when    **2** then    **3** Luckily    **4** after
**5** Suddenly    **6** finally

**2** *Sample answer*

Sam was both anxious and excited when he left the house. He and his brother got into the car and drove to the mountains because today was the first time he was going to compete in a snowboarding competition.

When they arrived, he put on his helmet and gloves and went to the start of the race. He heard the bell and went down the mountain. He was snowboarding very well, and he was feeling confident, when suddenly he fell. His leg really hurt, and he couldn't move. A doctor came and said, 'I think you've broken a bone.' She called a helicopter, which took him to hospital. Poor Sam! He couldn't walk for six weeks.

# Unit 10
## Reading Part 2

**1** E   **2** H   **3** D   **4** A   **5** F

## Vocabulary

**1**
**1** meal   **2** main   **3** courses   **4** dish   **5** food
**6** dessert   **7** products   **8** light

**2**
**1** library   **2** garage   **3** bakery / baker's
**4** chemist's / pharmacy   **5** bookstore / bookshop
**6** hairdresser's   **7** dentist's   **8** dry cleaner's

**3**
**1** borrow   **2** book   **3** make   **4** buy   **5** complain

## Grammar

**1**
**1** have my car cleaned
**2** have their kitchen painted
**3** has her shopping brought
**4** are having their wedding cake made
**5** have a photo of the family taken
**6** have her meals prepared

**2**
**1** think   **2** Don't invite   **3** accept   **4** Send
**5** Buy   **6** Make   **7** don't forget

## Listening Part 1

**1** C   **2** A   **3** B   **4** C   **5** A   **6** B   **7** C

---

**Track 11**

**Narrator:** For each question, choose the correct answer.

**1**
**Narrator:** What was the man unhappy with at the restaurant?
**Man:** You know, I don't think I'll go back to that new restaurant again.
**Woman:** Why's that? I heard it was quite good.
**Man:** Well, actually the food wasn't bad. We had some delicious chicken and chips, but the service wasn't great. They took ages to bring our meal, and when we complained, the waiter said he was very busy. When we finally got the bill it wasn't too expensive, but we'd been there for *two hours*.

---

**2**
**Narrator:** Where is the girl going?
**Girl:** Hi Dad, I'm just calling you to let you know my plans. You know I wanted to go to the concert this evening? Well, it's been cancelled, so Lily and I thought we'd go shopping. There's a new music shop in the shopping centre, not far from the hairdresser's where Mum goes. I want to get something for Richard's birthday. The thing is, it's raining a lot now. Can you pick me up outside the shopping centre at 8.30? Please!

**3**
**Narrator:** What did the man forget?
**Man:** I didn't think it would be so hot today. I'm boiling.
**Woman:** You really should wear something on your head. The sun is very strong.
**Man:** I know, I put my cap out next to my rucksack this morning, but now I can't find it.
**Woman:** Have you looked in the side pocket where you've got your water bottle?
**Man:** Ah yes, it's here. But my sunglasses aren't.
**Woman:** Well, the cap will protect your eyes a bit anyway.
**Man:** I suppose so, but it's annoying I left them at home.

**4**
**Narrator:** What does the man want to borrow?
**Man:** Hi Zoe. How's things?
**Woman:** Fine. What a surprise!
**Man:** Well, er, I'm calling to ask you a favour.
**Woman:** Yeah sure, what is it?
**Man:** Have you got a sleeping bag I could use? I'm going on a camping trip. My sister's lent me her cooking equipment, so I've got everything else.
**Woman:** I suppose so, but you will give it back, won't you? I think you've still got the torch I lent you two months ago.
**Man:** Oh dear, I'm sorry. I'll give both things back after the trip, I promise.

**5**
**Narrator:** How much will the woman pay for the meal?
**Woman:** That was an amazing meal! Let's get the bill, shall we?
**Man:** OK. ... Excuse me, could we have the bill, please?
**Waiter:** Here you are, sir. That'll be £45.40.
**Woman:** Right, so we'll pay half each. Let me do the maths. That's umm £22.70, then.
**Man:** I had a dessert, so I'll put in £5 more. Your share is £17.70.
**Woman:** That seems fair. It isn't expensive at all here, is it?

**6**
**Narrator:** Where does the man need to go first this afternoon?
**Woman:** Do you want to meet for a coffee this afternoon? I haven't seen you for ages.
**Man:** I'd love to, but I've got lots to do. I've got to meet my younger brother straight after he finishes school and take him to have his hair cut, and we have to go to the shopping centre before that to get him some new trainers.
**Woman:** What about later on then? We could have a pizza instead?
**Man:** That sounds like a good plan.

**7**
**Narrator:** Which film does the reviewer recommend?
**Reviewer:** There are three new films on at the Central cinema this week. *West Texas* is a classic cowboy movie, but I was disappointed by the story, which had no new ideas. If you're a fan of science fiction, as I am, then you'll love *The Time Traveller* with its adventures of a boy who finds himself living on the moon. The film *Happy Day* follows the life of a footballer, which some people might enjoy – I found it rather long.

## Writing Part 2 (An article)

**1**
**1** c   **2** a, f, i   **3** e   **4** d, g   **5** b, h

**2**
No, he didn't answer about the amount of sleep.

**3** *Sample answer*

Everyone knows it is important to have a healthy lifestyle because then you have a better life and enjoy yourself.

If you sleep well for enough time, you wake up feeling good. Exercise is essential as well. You should walk everywhere if you can and doing a sport is good for your mind and body.

I think the most important way to be healthy is to eat the right food. You should have a diet that includes different types of food and drink lots of water.

If you can eat well sleep enough and have fun doing exercise, you will be healthy and happy.

## Unit 11
## Listening Part 4

**1**
**1** C   **2** B   **3** A   **4** B   **5** A   **6** B

---

**Track 12**
**Narrator:** For each question, choose the correct answer. You will hear an interview with a young man from Bermuda called Magnus, who helps protect the oceans and the wildlife in them.
**Interviewer:** Today we're talking to Magnus Henneberger, who lives on Bermuda, an island in the Mid-Atlantic. So Magnus, when did you first become interested in the sea and marine wildlife?
**Magnus:** Well, we'd been reading about it in class at school. Then someone from an environmental organisation came and gave a presentation about the amount of plastic in the ocean and what they're trying to do about it. I was really impressed and registered to become a member.
**Interviewer:** What was the first thing you did after you joined the organisation?
**Magnus:** We had to go out on a paddle board – that's like a surfboard – on a lake. We attached a kind of net to the board and collected plants and pieces of plastic. These went to a laboratory to be tested in order to find out which things were contaminating the water.
**Interviewer:** What did you learn from this?

---

**Magnus:** We found very small pieces of plastic called microbeads that are used in everyday things like toothpaste and skin-care products. These aren't thrown away. We use them on ourselves and they get into water when we wash. We think these won't hurt anything because we use them on our bodies, but the plastic gets into rivers and is washed out to sea. This is very dangerous because marine animals, especially fish, eat them and sometimes die, and if humans eat contaminated animals they can become ill as well.
**Interviewer:** What advice would you give people about helping to protect marine life?
**Magnus:** I've actually started a campaign to tell people not to buy some beauty products. When you buy creams and liquids, check on the label that they are not made with microbeads. It's better to have less smooth skin than end up with no life in the sea.
**Interviewer:** So, what has been your greatest achievement so far?
**Magnus:** We have regular beach-cleaning days, and I think we're beginning to make a difference, but I felt most proud when our local aquarium decided to display my sculpture. I'd made it from objects that I'd collected on the beach. Now all the tourists that visit can see how we're polluting our planet.
**Interviewer:** And what do you want to do next?
**Magnus:** Well, there are some charities which have some great environmental projects that I would love to take part in. But before that, of course, I need to get a degree in environmental science. Afterwards, I would love to come back to the island and carry on my work here.
**Interviewer:** Thank you, Magnus, and good luck!

## Grammar

**1**
**1** was stolen          **2** aren't used          **3** were woken up
**4** are often hunted    **5** was watched          **6** was created
**7** wasn't blown down   **8** are protected

**2**
**1** When was the aquarium built?
**2** When was the environmental organisation set up?
**3** Where is the rubbish taken for recycling? / Where is the rubbish for recycling taken?
**4** When were the results given to the students?
**5** What are the machines used for?
**6** How are the animals captured?
**7** Were you brought up in the countryside?
**8** Are the animals well looked after / looked after well in the zoo? / Are the animals in the zoo well looked after / looked after well?

**3**
**1** is ('s) used        **2** is ('s) not protected    **3** were cut down
**4** was built           **5** was set up               **6** were picked up
**7** are not / aren't prevented                          **8** is ('s) read

**4**
**1** When was **that photograph taken**?   **2** paint → painted   **3** ~~was~~
**4** ~~been~~   **5** ~~writen~~ → written   **6** garden **is** / **was** surrounded

**5**
**1** the fastest         **2** better        **3** more quietly
**4** more carefully      **5** more slowly   **6** more easily
**7** the hardest         **8** the worst

## Vocabulary

### 1

| | | | | | | | | K |
|---|---|---|---|---|---|---|---|---|
| | P | E | N | G | U | I | N | A |
| T | | C | | O | | | | N |
| I | | A | | S | | | | G |
| G | | M | | T | | | | A |
| E | | E | | R | | | | R |
| R | F | L | A | M | I | N | G | O |
| | | | R | | C | | | O |
| | E | L | E | P | H | A | N | T |

**1** elephant    **2** camel    **3** flamingo    **4** tiger
**5** ostrich    **6** penguin    **7** bear    **8** kangaroo

### 2
**1** confirmation    **2** discussion    **3** invitation
**4** Pollution    **5** replacement    **6** translation
**7** excitement    **8** development    **9** reservation
**10** exploration

### 3
**1** announcement    **2** education    **3** completion
**4** inventions    **5** disappointment    **6** entertainment

## Reading Part 5

**1** D    **2** A    **3** C    **4** A    **5** B    **6** C

## Writing Part 1

### 1
**1** that I have a few days off
**2** accept the invitation; which activity you prefer; why I don't need boots; a suggestion about something else to do

### 2
**1** I'd love    **2** haven't had    **3** did    **4** have already grown
**5** love    **6** is    **7** I'll be

### 3
No, he forgot to mention the boots.

**4** *Sample answer*

Hi Freddie,

Thanks for your invitation for this weekend. It's a brilliant idea! It will be great to see you after so long.

I'd like to do both activities with the environmental club, but it might be more fun to work in the river because we can see more wildlife there. Are there any fish? I don't need to borrow boots since I've got special ones that I use for fishing.

On Saturday night we could go out to eat. I'd like to invite you to a good dinner! There's an excellent Italian restaurant near your house, isn't there?

See you soon!

Cheers,

## Unit 12
## Listening Part 3

**1** (TV) studio    **2** May    **3** beauty
**4** clothes    **5** show    **6** using lights

---

**Track 13**

**Narrator:** For each question, write the correct answer in the gap. Write one or two words or a number or a date or a time. You will hear a woman called Jemma talking about a video-making course she went on last year.

**Woman:** It all began when I met someone at a party who invited me to go to see him at work in a TV studio. While I was there, the camera operator let me try filming and it was amazing, so the next day I went to the camera shop as soon as I got up to buy a cheap video camera.

I wanted to learn more, so I decided to sign up for a film course at the weekends. The course was every Saturday morning from 10 till 2. It lasted from September to May with a break in December, and then we had some extra sessions in the afternoon when we reached the final month of the course.

We worked in groups. I was with some really nice people and we created all kinds of productions, like giving beauty tips, teaching dance routines and writing and performing our own comic plays or short dramas.

We didn't need any experience or equipment – they had enough computers for us to share and cameras for each group. The only thing we had to bring was any special clothes we needed. I remember I borrowed several things from my elderly aunt!

At the end of the course, I got a certificate to show I had learnt basic video production skills, and we did a show for friends and relatives, so they could see the work we'd been doing. That was probably the best moment, when I could see how people enjoyed what we had created.

I'd really recommend this course to anyone who wants to find out about making great video clips. I wasn't very good at dancing or speaking in front of the camera, but I'd like to improve my skills at using lights, so I'm sure I'll do another course soon.

---

## Vocabulary

### 1
**1** check / see / look at    **2** call / phone    **3** play    **4** take
**5** go    **6** share    **7** text    **8** play / listen to

### 2
**1** tell    **2** speak    **3** said    **4** talk    **5** ask for
**6** say    **7** tell    **8** talk

### 3
**1** impolite    **2** incomplete    **3** impatient
**4** unbelievable    **5** incorrect    **6** impossible
**7** uncomfortable    **8** inexpensive    **9** unfriendly

## Reading Part 4

**1** C    **2** H    **3** A    **4** E    **5** F

# Grammar

**1**
1 (that) we couldn't leave   2 (that) he didn't want
3 (that) they were leaving   4 (that) Zoe would come
5 (that) Harry had lived   6 (that) she had ('d) enjoyed

**2**
1 Are you going to China?
2 When will you give me a day off?
3 How many people has Mia invited to the party?
4 Do you want to go to the beach?
5 Why can't you stay longer?
6 Where did you buy that dress?

**3**
1 to write clearly
2 not to use a pen
3 to be careful with spelling
4 not to worry about understanding every word
5 to guess the meaning
6 not to forget to bring an identification document

**4**
1 ~~said~~ → told   2 ~~can~~ → could   3 ~~to~~   4 ~~told~~ → asked
5 ~~don't~~ → not to   6 **had** found

**5**
1 what time it is                   2 I can/could take a photo
3 where the IT department is   4 how often you look at your phone
5 where Thomas lives

## Writing Part 2 (A story)

**1**
C   A   B

**2**
1 Lucas said, 'I've hurt my leg.'
2 The police officer asked, 'When did you arrive home?'
3 Marina announced, 'I'm going to America.'
4 Charlie replied, 'I don't know.'

**3**
1 Lucas said (that) he had hurt his leg.
2 The police officer asked when I/we had arrived home.
3 Marina announced (that) she was going to America.
4 Charlie replied (that) he didn't know.

**4** *Sample answer*

I slowly opened the box and looked inside. There was nothing there! I felt disappointed because I had expected a present for my birthday.

My wife was watching me. She smiled and told me to look more carefully. Then I saw a tiny envelope. I quickly opened it and read the note inside. It said 'Look outside.' I immediately ran to the window and looked out.

At the front of the house I saw a brand-new black motorbike. I was amazed. I hugged my wife and said, 'Thank you. This is the best present ever! Let's go for a ride.'

## Vocabulary extra
### Unit 1

**1**
**Across: 1** armchair   **5** hall   **9** cupboard   **11** kitchen   **14** sofa
**15** garage   **16** toilet
**Down: 2** cushion   **3** blanket   **4** balcony   **6** wardrobe   **7** cooker
**8** bath   **10** stairs   **12** chest   **13** bedroom

**2**
1 cupboard   2 furniture   3 mirror   4 dining
5 drawers   6 kitchen

**3**
1 on   2 at   3 at   4 on   5 at   6 in

## Unit 2

**1**
**Across:**   2 staff   4 quit   7 employee   9 retire   11 gap
12 experience
**Down:**   1 business   3 accommodation   5 apply   6 degree
8 form   10 career

**2**
1 failed        2 learned / learnt        3 passed        4 took
5 missed      6 set off                    7 studied      8 taught

**3**
1 took,  passed      2 set off, missed      3 studied, failed
4 taught, learned / learnt

**4**
1 ~~do~~ → make         2 ~~make~~ → / have      3 ~~pass~~ → spend
4 ~~learned~~ → taught   5 ~~made~~ → took        6 ~~lose~~ → miss

**5**
A 1, 4, 7, 8            B 3, 5, 9            C 2, 6

## Unit 3

**1**
1 chain, helmet        2 bake, recipe        3 brush, watercolours
4 fire, sleeping bag   5 digital, cameras   6 practise, performance
7 queen, board        8 water, wetsuit

**2**
A **4**   B **8**   C **6**   D **5**   E **7**   F **2**   G **1**   H **3**

**3**
1 feel like / fancy, look forward to        2 suggest
3 take, afford        4 remember, promise   5 run out of, finish
6 fancy / feel like, go off                 7 put down, enjoy

## Unit 4

**1**
1 good time        2 dry                      3 hire
4 snorkelling      5 peace and quiet        6 trip
7 sightseeing      8 market                  9 souvenirs
10 original        11 journey                12 hang

**2**
**Across: 3** palace   **5** hall   **8** monument   **9** youth   **10** camping
**Down: 1** sports   **2** department   **4** gallery   **6** factory   **7** fountain

## Unit 5

**1**
1 miserable        2 cheerful        3 annoyed
4 confused        5 surprised       6 embarrassed
7 frightened      8 jealous

**2**
**Positive:** brave, cute, funny, generous, grateful, pleased, satisfied
**Negative:** afraid, angry, ashamed, bored, depressed, disappointed, guilty

**3** *Suggested answers*
| | | |
|---|---|---|
| **1** boring | **2** cute | **3** angry |
| **4** guilty | **5** generous | **6** grateful |
| **7** brave | **8** satisfying | |

**4**
| | | | |
|---|---|---|---|
| **1** tiring | **2** surprised | **3** frightening | **4** relaxing |
| **5** amazed | **6** confusing | | |

**5**
| | | | | | |
|---|---|---|---|---|---|
| **1** about | **2** of | **3** about | **4** with | **5** by | **6** of |

## Unit 6

**1**
**Across: 1** fair  **7** interval  **9** screen  **11** director
**12** entertainment
**Down: 2** audience  **3** admission  **4** stage  **5** review  **6** series
**8** book **10** row

**2**
| | | | |
|---|---|---|---|
| **1** opera | **2** live | **3** chat | **4** crowd |
| **5** scenery | **6** ballet | | |

**3**
| | | | |
|---|---|---|---|
| **1** found out | **2** gone | **3** met | **4** known |
| **5** got to know | **6** been | | |

## Unit 7

**1**
| | | |
|---|---|---|
| **1** roundabout | **2** railway | **3** underground |
| **4** car park | **5** thunderstorm | **6** traffic jam |

**2**
| | | |
|---|---|---|
| **1** roundabout | **2** underground | **3** railway |
| **4** thunderstorms | **5** car park | **6** traffic jam |

**3**
**1** B  **2** D  **3** E  **4** A  **5** C

## Unit 8

**1**
**1** f  **2** e  **3** a  **4** c  **5** d  **6** b

**2**
| | | | |
|---|---|---|---|
| **1** noisy | **2** cheerful | **3** modern | **4** lazy |
| **5** old-fashioned | **6** polite | **7** miserable | **8** rude |

**3**
| | | | |
|---|---|---|---|
| **1** confident | **2** generous | **3** selfish | **4** quiet |
| **5** anxious | **6** kind | **7** shy | |
| word in grey: friends | | | |

**4**
| | | | |
|---|---|---|---|
| **1** Danny | **2** short, dark, curly | **3** Jamie | **4** Jamie |
| **5** long, dark | **6** straight/short, blonde | **7** Sara, Danny | |
| **8** Jamie | | | |

**5**
| | | | |
|---|---|---|---|
| **1** made up | **2** grew up | **3** get on | **4** ran out of |

## Unit 9

**1**
| | | |
|---|---|---|
| **1** cut | **2** high temperature | **3** operation |
| **4** medicine | **5** plaster cast | **6** bandage |

**2**
| | | | |
|---|---|---|---|
| **1** go | **2** track | **3** scored | **4** court |
| **5** went | **6** hit | **7** do | **8** gym |
| **9** pitch | **10** beat | | |

**3** *Suggested answers*
**1** helmet – cycling, ice hockey, American football
**2** bat – table tennis, cricket, baseball
**3** kit – Most sports have their own 'kit'.
**4** net – tennis, badminton, volleyball
**5** trainers – athletics, running
**6** swimsuit – swimming, beach volleyball, diving
**7** racket – tennis, badminton, squash
**8** gloves – skiing, snowboarding, football (goalkeeper)

## Unit 10

**1**
**Across**
**2** customer  **4** teeth  **5** library  **7** bakery / baker's
**10** hairdresser  **11** bill  **12** chef
**Down**
**1** bargain  **3** vegetarian  **6** butcher  **8** chemist  **9** garage

**2**
| | | | | |
|---|---|---|---|---|
| **1** mended | **2** borrow | **3** complained | **4** made | **5** book |

**3** *Suggested answers*
**Proteins:** beef, cheese, chicken, eggs, peanuts, steak, tuna
**Carbohydrates:** bread, cake, chips, pasta, rice
**Fruit & vegetables:** apple, cucumber, grapes, lettuce, mushrooms, pear, spinach
**Milk & dairy products:** butter, cheese, yoghurt
**Fats & sugars:** butter, cake, chocolate, sweets

**4**
| | | | |
|---|---|---|---|
| **1** jug | **2** fork | **3** spoon | **4** frying pan |
| **5** knife | **6** glass | **7** chopsticks | **8** plate |

## Unit 11

**1**
| | | |
|---|---|---|
| **1** cliff | **2** hill | **3** beach |
| **4** island | **5** rock | **6** wood |
| **7** lake | **8** valley | **9** stream |
| **10** waterfall | | |

**2**
| | | |
|---|---|---|
| **1** pollution | **2** solar | **3** wild |
| **4** waste | **5** protect | **6** danger |
| **7** save | **8** aims | |

**3**
| | | |
|---|---|---|
| **1** announcement | **2** discussion | **3** creation |
| **4** excitement | **5** enjoyment | **6** invitation |
| **7** education | **8** reduction | |

## Unit 12

**1**
| | | | |
|---|---|---|---|
| **1** lies | **2** an email | **3** your manager | |
| **4** speak | **5** meaning | **6** slang | **7** say  **8** ask |

**2**
**1** c  **2** f  **3** g  **4** d  **5** h  **6** a  **7** b  **8** e

**3**
| | | | |
|---|---|---|---|
| **1** unhealthy | **2** patient | **3** unfair | **4** polite |
| **5** expensive | **6** unsuccessful | **7** perfect | **8** incomplete |

## Acknowledgements

**The authors and publishers acknowledge the following sources of copyright material and are grateful for the permissions granted. While every effort has been made, it has not always been possible to identify the sources of all the material used, or to trace all copyright holders. If any omissions are brought to our notice, we will be happy to include the appropriate acknowledgements on reprinting and in the next update to the digital edition, as applicable.**

Key: U = Unit

### Text

**U3:** Megan Knowles-Bacon for the text and listening material. Reproduced with kind permission of Megan Knowles-Bacon; **U8:** Flawsome Brands Ltd for the text about Maciek Kacprzyk and Karina Sudenyte. Reproduced with permission of Maciek Kacprzyk and Karina Sudenyte.

### Photography

The following images are sourced from Getty Images.

**U1**: AndreyPopov/iStock/Getty Images Plus; Sapsiwai/iStock/Getty Images Plus; FG Trade/iStock/Getty Images Plus; Patricia Hamilton/Moment; **U2**: Matteo Colombo/Moment; Tetra Images; filadendron/E+; Tom Werner/DigitalVision; ViewStock; **U3**: leaf/iStock/Getty Images Plus; Creative Crop/Photodisc; **U4**: Cultura RM Exclusive/Gary John Norman; Bernd Vogel/Corbis; Ian Cumming/Axiom Photographic Age; Atlantide Phototravel/Corbis Documentary; **U5**: skynesher/E+; Martin Dimitrov/E+; Geber86/E+; Peopleimages/E+; **U6**: Hill Street Studios/Blend Images; Westend61; Hero Images; Caiaimage/Sam Edwards; Dimitri Otis/Photographer's Choice; **U7**: fotog; Simon Marcus Taplin/Corbis; FokinOl/iStock/Getty Images Plus; BJI; **U8**: Jupiterimages/Stockbyte; Axel Bueckert/EyeEm; Westend61; Manfred Gerber/EyeEm; ByeByeTokyo/E+; amriphoto/E+; ermingut/iStock/Getty Images Plus; **U9**: Ross Woodhall/Cultura; ImageDB/iStock/Getty Images Plus; mbbirdy/iStock Unreleased; Manuel-F-O/iStock/Getty Images Plus; imagenavi; pic_studio/iStock/Getty Images Plus; InterestingLight/iStock/Getty Images Plus; Alex Ortega/EyeEm; supermimicry/iStock Unreleased; Jordan Mansfield/Stringer/Getty Images Sport; **U10**: FangXiaNuo/E+; baona/E+; Dougal Waters/DigitalVision; Ranta Images/iStock/Getty Images Plus; Westend61; JGI/Jamie Grill/Blend Images; **U11**: apomares/iStock/Getty Images Plus; Moment; Nigel Pavitt/AWL Images; Robert Daly/Caiaimage; **U12**: bjones27/E+; WLDavies/E+; Caiaimage/Paul Bradbury; timsa/E+.

### Vocabulary Extra

**U1**: Hybrid Images/Cultura; **U3**: Caiaimage/Rafal Rodzoch; **U4**: cinoby/iStock/Getty Images Plus; **U6**: Hybrid Images/Cultura; **U7**: Katsutoshi Yahata/EyeEm; Hans Blossey/imageBROKER; chictype/iStock/Getty Images Plus; Gail Shotlander/Moment; Boris Jordan Photography/Moment; fotog; **U9**: Peter Dazeley/Photographer's Choice; Stephen Oliver/Dorling Kindersley; Westend61; Kameleon007/iStock/Getty Images Plus; talevr/iStock/Getty Images Plus; rolleiflextlr/iStock/Getty Images Plus; Vevchic86/iStock/Getty Images Plus; **U12**: jamtoons/DigitalVision Vectors.

The following images are sourced from other sources.

**U3**: © Mark Hesketh-Jennings/Megan Knowles-Bacon; **U8**: © Flawsome! Drinks.

Front cover photography by Yagi Studio/Taxi Japan/Getty Images.

### Illustrations

Amerigo Pinelli; Abel Ippolito.

### Audio

Produced by Leon Chambers and recorded at The SoundHouse Studios, London

### Page make up

emc design ltd